BIG AUDACIOUS MEANING

Unleashing Your Purpose-Driven Story

By Dan Salva

Big Audacious Meaning – Unleashing Your Purpose-Driven
Story
Dan Salva

Published in the United States by Create Thrust Publishing
ISBN 978-1-7329432-0-9

For Amy,
who laughs with me.

CONTENTS

INTRODUCTION

When we are in our 20's, we're filled with ambition and a fervor for starting a career. The 30's and 40's find us raising families, climbing the corporate ladder, and maybe even starting a business – pursuing professional success. And then, the 50's roll around. The peak earning years.

This is the time when most are in a higher wage bracket. The kids are moving out and with them goes financial obligations for tuition, insurance, and groceries. Oh, and did I mention groceries? There is the potential to leverage years of experience and hard-earned wisdom to command a higher income - while having expenses shrink at the same time.

But then comes this tug.

Some want us to believe it comes from desperation. That those in their 50's are realizing that they'll never be gazillionaires. Or rock stars. I don't buy it. I do believe that we start to sense our mortality. That we start to understand our time is limited. And that we want to make the most of it.

We feel the shift from the material to the ethereal.

That leads us to think about how we use our time. We think about our contribution. Will we spend that time absorbed in our own self-gratification? Or will we use it for something more fulfilling? Will we spread some good?

This isn't reserved for just this stage of life. We all experience it in varying degrees at varying ages.

We all have an altruistic side. We have a need to give back. To serve our fellow man. It may ebb and flow. But at some point, it becomes undeniable. We can't push it aside or put it off. So what do we do about it?

The limits of time and treasure

If you're like me, what you'd like to be able to do outpaces your resources. Somewhere between paying bills and saving for the future lies the amount you can contribute to a cause. Somewhere between your work hours and the family obligations lies the time you can volunteer.

We have two finite assets - time and treasure. The amount of good we can do is equal to the amount of our time and treasure we have to give. Let's face it, there is only so much money and so much time in the day to give. Which leads to two options:

1. We could wait until we have amassed large sums of wealth (some time in the distant future) and then we could really give.
2. We could all quit our jobs and go to work for a not-for-profit. Cash in our 401(k)s and give it all away.

Needless to say, I struggled with both these scenarios. It made me think that there had to be something I was missing.

And then I started to think about all those work hours.

I thought about all the organizations where all of us work and the thousands of lives they touch.

A question started to form.

What if we could help those organizations clarify the larger purpose that they serve? What if we could help them see the profound effect they could have on an individual life? A community? The world? We wouldn't be limited by our individual time and treasure to spread more goodness in the world.

This wouldn't be at the expense of growth or profit. No, people love organizations that demonstrate this kind of purpose. They flock to them. Because they have meaning. And that is something that is in short supply in today's over-amped, over-hyped, and over-accelerating world. We can give people the opportunity to align with that meaning.

Crazy? You can call it that, but I'd prefer to call it Big Audacious Meaning.

Imagine the difference we can make in those thousands of lives – simply by clarifying that Big Audacious Meaning that is at the core. Imagine the profound effect it could have.

As I started to think more and more about this, I realized that this was my own Big Audacious Meaning. To exponentially amplify the amount of goodness I could spread in the world by helping others do the same.

And so, that is why this book is here today.

SECTION 1: THE MAGIC OF A BIG AUDACIOUS MEANING

CHAPTER 1
The nature of purpose

A company can develop a vision. It can declare its mission. These can be lofty and ambitious. Yet, they rarely elicit a visceral reaction. You know that feeling. When something connects so powerfully with you that your heart starts beating a little faster. There's no calculated evaluation at this point. There is just a rush of adrenaline.

So few organizations stop to examine this. Most will put together a serviceable mission and then quickly move on to tweaking the tangible things. At some point, the results of the tweaking start to diminish. Management goes on a retreat to ponder why there is very little passion associated with their brand. Whether it's the lack of passion among their customers or their team members.

How purpose forms

Companies start because somebody sees an opportunity. Maybe it's to do something new. Serve an unmet need. Or maybe it's to improve the way something is already being done. Most of the time, this person has a belief that he or she has a better way of doing things.

Ian Percy sums it up in his book *The Profitable Power of Purpose*, "I don't know your company or its history. But I guarantee that it was started by someone who was irritated about something."[1]

Common to these entrepreneurs is the belief that they could

provide something of value. And many times, they have a belief that they could make a real difference in the world.

This story can be very compelling. After all, it was powerful enough to cause the company founders to go out on a limb. Maybe even to leave a comfortable job to pursue this idea.

This story should be at the very core of the brand.

When I started my business in 1996, I believed the marketing and advertising industry needed more transparency and common sense. Since those things seemed to be in short supply, we called what we delivered "uncommonsense". We believed that uncommonsense could transform the way organizations did business. So, this became the story from our beginning that formed our brand.

Sometimes the story gets lost. A company evolves. Leadership changes. And then changes again. The founders' original story becomes a footnote in the company's history.

I've worked with organizations that have lost their way. Either they no longer had a clear picture of what they stood for, or they had some vague notion that didn't do much to inspire anyone.

Many times I've dug into a company's history to discover that original story. To uncover that original passion. Reconnecting with that can infuse the organization with a meaning and purpose that has been lost. Employees start to feel like they are part of something larger than themselves – something meaningful and worth caring about. And customers and prospects suddenly are more likely to become evangelists for the brand.

That's what getting back to its origins can do for an organization.

Sometimes the company has changed so significantly that the

original story no longer applies.

I worked with a minerals company that morphed pretty significantly over a century of acquisitions and evolutions. If you asked their people what they did, they'd tell you they operated salt mines.

You know that saying that people use when they're headed off to work:

"Well, it's off to the old salt mines."

That was literally what these people did. The thing is, mining salt in and of itself was not its compelling, purpose-driven story. As we worked through the process, the real purpose emerged. You see, that salt was shipped up and down the Mississippi River to towns that used it to keep the roads free of ice and snow during the winter. These towns depended on that salt. In fact, studies even showed that you could actually attribute a significant reduction in the number of accidents to the application of that salt to the streets, and a reduction in the number of weather-related deaths on the roads.

Now that was a compelling story. Think about it. Who would you rather work for? A company that mines a commodity product? Or, a company that helps save lives?

That story became the foundation for the purpose of the organization and the reinvention of the brand.

Defining a purpose starts with a compelling and meaningful story. It may be in our history. Or it may be waiting to be revealed in what we do today.

Just know that it's more than what we do or how we do it. That's stuff people want to know, but it's not why they care. They care when we share our larger purpose and show them how that purpose helps make a difference in their lives and their world. And we get bonus points when we invite them to become part of that effort to make a difference.

Create that and we'll give birth to something extraordinary. A brand that gives our people and prospects something they can believe in and care about.

Push vs. pull

There is a concept in business planning introduced decades ago by Jim Collins and Jerry Porras, authors of *Built to Last: Successful Habits of Visionary Companies*. It's called the Big Hairy Audacious Goal (BHAG).[2]

Every viable organization sets goals. Usually, these are reasonably attainable, taking into account past performance, market conditions and more. They may be expressed as something like, "Increase sales by x% over the next two quarters." While these types of goals are important for any organization, they simply can't do what a BHAG can do – help an organization really see what it is capable of achieving. That's why BHAGs are often referred to as stretch goals.

A BHAG serves as a catalyst to drive progress. It can empower an organization to reach past what it feels comfortable achieving. When properly communicated and managed, it can motivate everyone to push himself or herself.

It's interesting that when we talk about the effort to achieve something beyond the expected, we talk about "pushing" ourselves. It's doing something that falls outside of what we would be compelled to do naturally. This is why the BHAG is valuable. It gives us a reason to challenge ourselves. At the outset, people get excited about the prospects of doing something extraordinary. So there is energy and enthusiasm that surrounds the BHAG.

But what happens when things get tough? (And they will get tough.) It's easy to get beaten down and demoralized. Just imploring everyone to "push" and "challenge" himself or herself is not enough. In fact, at this point in time, it actually may be more demoralizing to tell people to just "work a little harder". It's too easy to give up and rationalize, "Well, it's not like we're failing – after all, it was a *stretch* goal."

This is the time that we need something that goes beyond "pushing". We need something that "pulls" us toward the goal with a magnetic force.

To be fair, Collins talked about the need for companies to have a purpose that drove the culture as well. And for good reason. A purpose can energize each of us to continually generate the motivation that will propel us to that big goal. I'm talking about a self-sustaining force that doesn't require something or someone to goad us to "push" ourselves, but rather, inspires us – harnessing our imagination and emotion to fuel our extraordinary efforts.

This meaning is something more than, "I hit that stretch goal." It is a belief that we are contributing to something larger than ourselves. And in the process, making a difference in the world around us. When people and organizations feel that, amazing things happen.

Enter the Big Audacious Meaning

Throughout this book I write about what purpose is (and what it is not.) Surprisingly, there is no universally acknowledged definition. On one end of the spectrum, you have Merriam-Webster, which defines purpose as, "Something set up as an object or end to be attained."[3] On the other end, we find lofty statements like, "It's why you exist." The first seems rather utilitarian and uninspired – really not coming close to describing the kind of profound potential that a purpose holds. The second would seem to hold the promise of deep meaning, but it just feels vague.

As I worked with organizations to nurture this potential over the years, I saw some common elements emerge time and time again. These elements inform a definition that feels both concrete and inspiring:

Purpose is the profound difference you can make in a life, a community, or even the world.

Today, this definition has become the touchstone. Each time we narrow in on clarifying a purpose with an organization, we ask questions like:

"Is it truly profound?"

"Will it make a meaningful difference in a life?'

"Could it transform a community?"

"Could it make the world a better place?"

It's been road-tested – being refined over hundreds of hours of work with purpose-seeking organizations. Over that time, it has even received its own special shorthand. It has come to be called Big Audacious Meaning.

Big Audacious Meaning gives this concept of purpose the sense of profoundness that it deserves.

It is more than a guiding principle. It is the fundamental belief that is at the core of the organization. A big belief that affects everyone our brand touches. Our believers, our prospects, our team members, our advocates and more.

It goes way beyond monthly goals and quarterly numbers. It lays claim to something audacious. And, it is full of meaning. Incredibly compelling and undeniably inspiring. It is the thing that gets all our believers up in the morning and keeps them motivated when things get challenging.

Big Audacious Meaning honors a fundamental need that we all have – to feel like our efforts mean something. To feel like their effect can ripple out into the lives of those around us.

Key Takeaways

- Many times, companies start because they have a belief that they could make a real difference in the world. This origin story can be very compelling and should be at the very core of the brand.

- Reconnecting with the company's origin story can infuse the organization with a meaning and purpose that has been lost.

- Sometimes the company has changed so significantly that the origin story no longer applies. In this case, a company needs to clarify the purpose it serves today.

- Purpose is more than what we do or how we do it. It's how we make a difference. It is different than a stretch goal. Stretch goals can challenge us to "push" ourselves. On the other hand, a purpose inspires us – it "pulls" us toward the goal.

- Big Audacious Meaning is a more compelling way to talk about purpose. It is defined as: the profound difference we can make in a life, a community, or even the world.

- A Big Audacious Meaning honors a fundamental need that we all have – to feel like our efforts mean something. To feel like their effect can ripple out into the lives of those around us.

CHAPTER 2
Sorting out the difference

Every once in awhile I'll meet someone who asks me what I do. I'll tell them that I help brands make a difference in the thousands of lives that they touch. And that I do it by helping organizations clarify their Big Audacious Meaning and then share it across the organization and across the world. I'm pretty passionate about this. Which makes my head want to explode when I hear, "Oh, we just redid our mission statement."

Argghhhh.

Now I could get all high and mighty and lecture on about how a mission is not a purpose. But usually, I simply ask, "Oh, what is it?" To which I get the response, "I don't remember."

The problem with the mission statement

It is undeniable that most mission statements are forgettable. There is something that feels monumentally wrong about that. "Mission" is a powerful word. A mission is aspirational. It describes how you will achieve your vision. Those are big, important things. They should be full of hope and crackling with energy. In fact, a mission is just this side of a quest. A journey of like-minded evangelists who are going to make a real difference in the world.

Unfortunately, most mission statements don't get anywhere near to generating that kind of ardor. They end up being littered with platitudes that do little to really inspire anyone. They become soulless expressions that nobody in the company can remember.

And since they are so vague and lofty, nobody quite knows what to do with them. Except put them on that page of the website that's buried three or four clicks in. Or frame them and put them on the wall of the boardroom where the only people who see them are the board members and the leadership team.

All of this is quite sad when you think about all the time and effort organizations spend on crafting their mission statements. I've been privy to my fair share of these exercises. 9 times out of 10 it's not a pretty thing to witness - a bunch of senior leaders debating the merit of one self-serving ambiguous phrase over another. Then emerging from the arduous and expensive process with something that will be hard for anybody to recall.

Inward vs. Outward

So what makes a Big Audacious Meaning different? Vision and mission statements talk about what the business will accomplish and how it will do it. They are all about the organization.

Imagine meeting someone and then having to listen to nothing but them talking about themselves. That's what too many mission statements do. They're inward facing. Add vague, corporate-speak to the mix and it's easy to see why 99% of mission statements feel generic. Like you could paste "Insert company name here" and it would work. It's also why nobody can remember them.

A Big Audacious Meaning, on the other hand, speaks to how we will make a difference for others. As a statement, it is selfless. It is us talking about those that we will serve.

Aspiring vs. Inspiring

As customers and prospects, we like how personal a Big Audacious

Meaning feels. It is easier and more inviting to engage because of that. Plus, we're more likely to care and be motivated because we want to see that purpose flourish.

Very few mission statements create that kind of fervor. So companies create programs to get team members excited about the mission. "To live it everyday" as they say. But should we really have to create a program to get everybody excited about the very thing that defines what is at our core? Shouldn't it already be so compelling that everyone can't help but feel energized by it? That's how it should be, right?

If we're creating an employee program to get them excited and engaged with the mission, we ought to take that as a sign that we have a problem.

This is why the mission statement should not be the all-powerful Oz of the organizational strategic framework. It's more like the Robin to the Batman that is purpose. Your Big Audacious Meaning should call the shots. It doesn't mean we don't need the mission statement. We just need to remember that it's the sidekick.

Vision and mission statements are an important part of how organizations articulate what they're all about. They act as inward-facing guideposts, providing the 'what' and 'how' to steer our efforts.

But understand the mission's role in relation to the purpose. Here is the hierarchy:

- **The Big Audacious Meaning (purpose)** – this is why we exist. It is the impact we will have on a life, a community, or even the world.

- **The vision** – this is what we hope to achieve that will help create that Big Audacious Meaning

- **The mission** – this is how we will achieve our vision

- **The values** – these are the principles that will guide us as we pursue our mission.

It's important to note that the Big Audacious Meaning sits above our vision, mission, and values.

If we treat it this way, we'll energize everyone from our team members to our prospects. We'll turn the mildly interested into the rabidly passionate. But we have to understand the dynamic. It's as simple as this: a mission statement is how we aspire. A Big Audacious Meaning is how we inspire.

Can a Big Audacious Meaning transform the vision, mission, and values?

In some regard, I myself had given up on vision, mission, and values. It was just too frustrating to get leadership teams to make these inspiring. Instead, I put my focus on helping organizations clarify their Big Audacious Meaning. Meaning is something everyone can get excited about. Leadership. Employees. Customers, prospects, and more. Then I had one of my clients surprise me. They asked if their newly developed Big Audacious Meaning could inform a reinvention of their vision, mission, and values.

Could it? Holy cow! Yes!

If we want to infuse meaning in our organization, we need to make sure it's reflected in our vision. Let it form our mission and guide our values. These are the foundational elements of who we are.

Seems so stupidly simple, right? Don't be fooled. It takes courage and determination to stay focused on the singular idea of meaning. It's easy for the leadership team to slide back into the sea of blandness that most organizations swim in when it comes to vision, mission, and values.

Here is what my client did.

- **Vision** - rather than talk about how they would profit, my client stated how their constituents would prosper.

- **Mission** - my client defined how they would serve all their constituents and by doing so, how their constituents would help them accomplish the mission.

- **Values** – rather than follow the practice of choosing a set of single words, my client chose to express the values in simple, three-word phrases. They were humble. Honest. And had a focus on serving. They were the perfect complement to the mission and vision.

Imagine what it would look like to align your vision, mission, and values with your purpose. Imagine the excitement this could foster in team members who see the commitment to making a difference in lives, communities, and the world. Imagine the clarity that would emerge and the compelling stories you could tell to customers and prospects. As my client understood, this instantly boosts the potential for the organization.

Does this mean that the vision, mission, and values could actually inspire everyone? Is that really possible?

Holy cow! Yes!

It's not your Corporate Social Responsibility program

I had a friend ask me, "So is a Big Audacious Meaning like when the cable company gets its employees to go out and volunteer to rehab a playground?"

My answer was pretty blunt. "No."

I'm going to be black and white on this issue because there is something very important to understand about a Big Audacious Meaning. It is not your Corporate Social Responsibility (CSR) program. It is not your charitable giving program. It is not corporate volunteering.

So what makes a Big Audacious Meaning different? Here is the critical point. Those CSR programs and efforts are all about the organization giving (selflessly) to society. The organization expects nothing in return. Oh you can argue that they generate goodwill and that goodwill comes back to the organization down the road. This is true. It's just vague. And as such, hard to measure. A Big Audacious Meaning introduces a different dynamic. It puts forth the idea that we can serve society while financially bettering our organization. So we can turn around and help everyone prosper even more while we prosper. That creates a virtuous circle (I refuse to call it a "win-win" - you're welcome). That's what a Big Audacious Meaning does. It brings together meaning and money.

Does that mean we should abandon those CSR programs? Absolutely not. Those are all good and noble things. And every company should keep doing them. In fact, the Big Audacious Meaning should guide those efforts. If there is a disconnect, we ought to seriously reconsider that charitable effort. Seriously. If we're giving money to the Society For The Preservation Of Society Preservationists, we should be able to look to our Big Audacious Meaning and decide if we should really be funding the group. Then we should look for opportunities to connect with organizations and causes that line up with why we do what we do.

Bringing together meaning and money

For years, it was as if meaning and money were polar opposites. Diametrically opposed. Light and dark. Good and evil. We had to decide which one we wanted.

Did we want to bring meaning into the world? Then be prepared to sacrifice money to do it.

Did we want to make a whole bunch of money? Well, then we needed to be willing to delay doing anything with meaning attached until we were independently wealthy and could become philanthropists.

What organizations and individuals are starting to discover is that they don't have to be mutually exclusive. This isn't just theory. There are some exciting examples of organizations that are embracing purpose and benefitting from it. One of the most well known is Unilever. Their purpose driven brands like Dove and Ben & Jerry's are growing at twice the pace of other brands in their portfolio.[4]

The problem is that purpose is at a bit of a disadvantage. Nobody says, "Purpose makes the world go round." It's money that gets the credit. Add to that the fact that purpose enjoys being associated with all the good qualities that causes it to get lumped in with not-for-profit efforts.

In order for the idea of purpose to grow, it needs to step outside the world of not-for-profits. Business needs to see that purpose leads to profit.

This is a critical point. Businesses will continue to have foundations and charitable programs. These are good things that should continue. But if we relegate purpose to this realm, it will never reach its full potential. It will always be that nice thing that a company does that really doesn't directly relate to the financial viability of the organization.

Purpose needs street cred. CFOs need to see the difference it makes in the numbers. Leaders need to view it as a measurable strategy for building high-quality, sustainable and expanding returns. Purpose needs to have an unassailable connection to the top and bottom lines. Only then will it be viewed as a critical asset and not just a nice thing to do.

Key Takeaways

- Most mission statements are forgettable – self-centered and littered with platitudes that do little to really inspire anyone. A Big Audacious Meaning is selfless. It is us talking about those that we will serve. A mission statement should be how we aspire, while a Big Audacious Meaning is how we inspire.

- Companies create programs to get team members excited about the mission. If we're creating an employee program to get team members excited about something that should be inspiring, we ought to take that as a sign that we have a problem.

- Aligning your vision, mission, and values with your purpose helps boost all your efforts.

- The Big Audacious Meaning is why we exist. The vision is what we hope to achieve that will help create that Big Audacious Meaning. The mission is how we will achieve our vision. The values are the principles that will guide us as we pursue our mission.

- A Big Audacious Meaning is not your Corporate Social Responsibility (CSR) program, charitable giving, or corporate volunteering. Those programs are all about the organization giving to society, expecting nothing in return. A Big Audacious Meaning is about serving society while financially bettering our organization. It brings together meaning and money.

- Unilever is proving the value of a Big Audacious Meaning. Its purpose-driven brands like Dove and Ben & Jerry's are growing at twice the pace of other brands in their portfolio.

SECTION 2: WHY IT'S NEEDED IN TODAY'S WORLD

CHAPTER 3
How we got to where we are

Profit seems to have a history of conjuring up feelings that are anything but altruistic. The most famous sentiment may be, "Money is the root of all evil."

I began my post-college career in the 80's. A time when Michael Douglas portraying Gordon Gecko in the movie *Wall Street* was telling us, "Greed is good." Popular culture glamorized making money. Lots of it. Often by any means possible. And, of course, we had Reaganomics - also known as trickle down economics. It was the theory that as the rich got richer their gains would help fund social programs. So, in other words, the money would trickle down to support the rest of society. Unfortunately, many who got rich during this time forgot the trickle-down part.

It wasn't a decade later and we were experiencing the Internet boom. People were starting online companies that had ridiculous valuations. The stranger part was that a lot of these companies had no clear path to profit. It didn't matter. Everyone was caught up in the frenzy to fund the next big Internet sensation. Greed fueled a lot of crazy investment. When the bubble burst, we had a host of Monday morning quarterbacks who told us, "Of course these companies failed. They had no sustainable plan."

In both of these periods, purpose was relegated to some corporate-sponsored social program that most companies grudgingly supported. In the rush to make money, the idea of serving a greater good simply got shoved aside.

Then came the event that topped the previous two. Less than a decade after the Internet bubble burst, we experienced the mortgage crisis. An event that would devastate long-standing financial institutions and throw the country into what became known as the Great Recession.

It was triggered by an era of money lust. People were taking out loans to buy homes they couldn't afford. Others were using their homes like an ATM. Cashing out their home equity to pay for vacations and cars.

Everyone just assumed that home prices would always go up. With that line of thinking, it meant that there would be no problem paying those loans back in the future.

What we didn't expect was the mortgage industry meltdown. Home values plummeted. And people had unprecedented debt with no way to pay it back. People defaulted on their loans. Some just walked away from their homes, leaving the properties to their mortgage companies and banks.

We had another effect as well. With money tight, people stopped buying things. And when people stopped buying things, companies started laying off workers. We started to realize that our economy was driven by the ability of all of us to spend.

What was perhaps most disconcerting is that people got indignant about not being able to have what they wanted. They acted as if it was their constitutional right that was being violated. They protested that the American Dream was being trampled.

All of this made me think of my grandfather who lived through the Great Depression. He never talked about what was owed to him because of his citizenship. He didn't whine and complain that he had to live through hard years. He believed it was up to him to make what he could of himself despite the trying times. And it wasn't just my grandfather. There were plenty others like him. Folks that believed that the American Dream wasn't some guarantee of having things. Rather, it was the opportunity to make the most of yourself.

In his 1931 book The Epic of America, James Truslow Adams defined the American Dream as, "...a dream of social order in which each man and each woman shall be able to attain to the fullest stature of which they are innately capable, and be recognized by others for what they are, regardless of the fortuitous circumstances of birth or position."[5]

What happened in the span of 80-some years that the idea of the American Dream got twisted? Did my grandfather and his generation have a greater connection to a sense of purpose?

One thing is for certain: these three periods of my career over the course of three decades did nothing but reinforce the idea that money was a dirty word. That profit was a necessary evil in our world.

The Great Recession rocked a lot of people's worlds. Older generations started to deal with the realization that retirements would have to be put on hold. People late into their careers suddenly found themselves unemployed. Kids saw their parents struggle. This younger generation entered the workforce jaded. They saw little sense in just making a buck in a system that could kick you out after decades of working for a company. The idea of choosing meaning over money started to affect how this generation looked at work. It had organizations scrambling to understand these mysterious new Millennials.

Let's blame the Millennials?

There has been much written about how work has changed. Companies have bemoaned a lack of worker loyalty. And individuals have complained about the lack of company commitment to the worker.

This shift has come about at the same time as the Millennial generation (the largest generation) has entered the workforce.

Some have theorized that this generation has been the cause of the change in attitude about work. They may be the first generation not expected to do better financially than their parents. This has led them to put less emphasis on financial gain and shift more emphasis to intangibles that could make work more fulfilling. Furthermore, they saw their parents rise to middle management with big companies, get downsized out of a job, and then struggle to find employment. This may have contributed to the change in attitude about loyalty to an organization.

Defining a career

With past generations, much more emphasis was given to building a career with a company. This is how we got the concept of "climbing the corporate ladder". The idea of changing jobs came with a negative connotation. And the thought of changing careers was rare at best. Careers are no longer measured by tenure with a company.

Research from Gallup confirms the trend. As a 2016 post explains, "A recent Gallup report on the Millennial generation reveals that 21% of Millennials say they've changed jobs within the past year, which is more than three times the number of non-Millennials who report the same. Gallup estimates that Millennial turnover costs the U.S. economy $30.5 billion annually."[6]

This could be attributed to the lack of engagement among a generation that hasn't experienced any other relationship between the business world and employees. As the same Gallup post reveals, "Gallup has found that only 29% of Millennials are engaged at work, meaning only about three in 10 are emotionally and behaviorally connected to their job and company."

Today, it is expected that people will change jobs multiple times. In days past, it signaled instability in a candidate. Now, changing jobs is associated with characteristics like boldness and motivation.

The alternative reward

If financial gains seem less likely, then it makes sense that people will look for other means of gratification from their work.

As people deal with this new normal, an interesting thing happens. Discussion starts to increase around the idea of purpose. Maybe it is the Millennials' desire for meaning in their work. Maybe it is the Baby Boomers resigning themselves to the fact that they won't be owning yachts and taking walks on beaches in their golden years. Maybe it is all this and more that leads us to thinking that we don't need cars and boats and vacation homes. That having a sense of purpose in our work and our lives is actually the most rewarding thing we could hope to attain.

Key Takeaways

- Over three decades, we experienced three greed-fueled eras – the greed-is-good 80's, the dot-com bubble at the end of the 90's, and the Great Recession in the 00's.

- These three eras fueled the sentiment that money was a dirty word. That profit was a necessary evil in our world.

- This affected Millennials' attitude toward work. Choosing meaning over money started to emerge.

- Today, it is expected that people will change jobs multiple times. In days past, it signaled instability in a candidate. Now, changing jobs is associated with characteristics like boldness and motivation.

- As people deal with this new normal, an interesting thing happens. Discussion starts to increase around the idea of purpose. People are waking up to the idea that having a sense of purpose in our work and our lives is actually the most rewarding thing we could hope to attain.

CHAPTER 4
What we're all dealing with today

So much has shifted over the past three decades. Our relationship with organizations has morphed. The access to and speed of information has changed radically. Our definition of success has evolved. These have played a major role in the burgeoning interest in purpose.

As we look at where we are today, it's worth examining the factors that continue to contribute to the increasing need for something that grounds and centers us.

A legacy of busyness

I read an account of a guy examining where he stood after 20 years in business. He had made decent money. Doing what his upbringing had taught him. Filling his days with activity.

As he stood at the two-decade mark, he came to the conclusion that he wasn't sure what he had been so busy doing all those years. And he was wondering if there was something more.

We see it throughout the business world. People wearing busyness like a badge. It's how we measure our worth. We must be valuable – after all, we are so very busy.

It doesn't help that many a manager affirms the illusion. Busyness = value. Do you want to be seen as valuable? Well then, maybe you should take on a little more. Maybe you should work a little longer. None of us wants to be seen as not valuable. Fear is a powerful force.

That sucks. One study shows that more than half of Americans are burned out and overworked.[7]

And by the way, busyness is a lousy metric. Sooner or later, someone will come in and engineer a solution that will automate or streamline what we do. Our busyness will decline. And so will our sense of the value. In short, busyness is an illusion. An illusion we buy into. Because we have our families to think about. Mortgages to pay. And groceries to buy.

When I started my professional career in the mid '80's, purpose wasn't really a thing. Business was business. Finding your purpose was some sort of quasi-spiritual fluff preached by leftover hippies. It had nothing to do with corporations and the churning of the wheels of commerce. Busyness was a measure of value.

Today, our hyper-connectivity is game changing. We no longer view ourselves as just another cog in a machine that we really don't understand. We're seeing the bigger picture. And it's creating a new expectation.

In short, it is no longer busyness as usual.

Information overload

We are assailed by an onslaught of information. According to research from USC Marshall School of Business, the average consumer has 74 gigabytes or 9 DVDs worth of data sent to them on an average day.[8]

One estimate suggests that the average person today is exposed to an amount of information each day that is equal to what a person in the 15th century was exposed to over his lifetime.[9]

This rapid acceleration in the flow of information to us has been enabled by our dramatically expanded access. Before cable and satellite TV, we had only a handful of channels. Today we have hundreds. And that's just one of the screens we have available to us. We have laptops, tablets, and smartphones. Each giving us constant access. Sometimes even pushing information to us through alerts and updates. We live in a 24/7 information access world.

This massive amount of information creates a much larger cognitive load for all of us. McGill University psychology professor Daniel Levitin illustrates the point for us in his book, *The Organized Mind: Thinking Straight in the Age of Information Overload.* "In 1976, there were 9,000 products in the average grocery store, and now it's ballooned to 40,000 products. And yet most of us can get almost all our shopping done in just 150 items, so you're having to ignore tens of thousands of items every time you go shopping," says Levitin.[10]

The things that call for our attention on a daily basis have expanded exponentially in my lifetime. I'm going to sound like an old-timer, but when I was a kid, video games weren't a thing (okay, Pong did appear on our TV sets while I was in my teens.) A social network was that group of kids from the neighborhood that hung out on the corner. And we had three channels on our TV (and my mom still yelled at us to turn it off and go outside to play.) Looking back, there was no way we could have predicted the massive assault on our attention that we accept as normal today.

Assaulting our senses

Your phone buzzes. It's a text. You stop what you're doing to answer it. You finish and it buzzes again. It's an update from a news site you follow. Then your laptop dings. A message from a teammate. Then a notification of an email in your inbox. Then your phone buzzes again.

Wait. There's more. I haven't even mentioned the updates and notifications from Twitter, Facebook, LinkedIn, Instagram, Slack, Snapchat, Pinterest, and…well, you get the idea.

According to the Harvard Business Review, "…a study commissioned by Hewlett-Packard reported that the IQ scores of knowledge workers distracted by e-mail and phone calls fell from their normal level by an average of 10 points..."[11]

We all use the phrase, "Pay attention." But we may not have stopped to consider just how appropriate that phrase is.

The increased burden on our decision-making mechanism means that we either need to ignore information or expend more of our energy digesting it.

It does take energy. Something we have a finite quantity of in any given day. Processing this expanded amount of information can lead to decision fatigue. In his book *Thinking, Fast And Slow,* The Nobel Prize winning psychologist Daniel Kahneman sheds light on the idea of the energy required for us to make conscious decisions in what he labels as System 2 mode of thought.[12] We have to expend energy in order to make a conscious decision. That is what we "pay out" of our finite store of energy that we have each day. There is a real cost to what we decide to process.

With the increase in information and a finite amount of energy to expend, it is no surprise that attention spans have decreased significantly. According to Statistic Brain, attention spans have dropped by nearly one-third, falling from 12 seconds in 2000 to just 8.25 seconds by 2015.[13]

We learn to cope. We make quicker decisions on what to investigate and what to discard. We have become miserly with our attention, protecting that precious energy that we have.

Grounding

All of this can leave us feeling a bit untethered. We find ourselves whipsawed by the things calling for our attention at an ever-increasing pace. We look at all the busyness it creates and we wonder what all of it is for. This is why purpose has become so valuable. It returns us to a sense of meaning. It gives all of us the grounding that we desperately need.

Key Takeaways

- In the past, we would wear our busyness like a badge. We would equate our value to how busy we were. But that's changing. We're starting to realize that it's a lousy metric. It's no longer busyness as usual.

- The average person today is exposed to an amount of information each day that is equal to what a person in the 15th century was exposed to over his lifetime. The assault on our attention has grown exponentially.

- Today's information overload actually has a negative affect on our IQ. Plus, processing this expanded amount of information can lead to decision fatigue. As we try to cope, attention spans have decreased by nearly one-third, falling from 12 seconds in 2000 to just 8.25 seconds by 2015.

- We find ourselves whipsawed by the things calling for our attention at an ever-increasing pace. Purpose has become valuable because it returns us to a sense of meaning. It gives all of us the grounding that we desperately need.

CHAPTER 5
Our desire for purpose, caring, and meaning

I was working on an internal initiative for a nationwide tax preparation firm. We were in search of stories that we could hold up as examples of team members living the mission. I remember thinking at the time that the mission wasn't all that inspiring. What is compelling about living a mildly interesting mission? How was I going to capture stories that would move people if the guiding principle wasn't really much to get excited about?

My job was to talk to tax preparers in the field. I don't know how you think about this, but I couldn't understand why anybody would want to be a tax preparer. Taxes are complicated. And boring. I don't want to think about taxes. Now I was supposed to interview a bunch of people that made this their life's pursuit. What could they tell me that would be even remotely inspiring?

Needless to say, this was an awful bias to take into an interview. There was another complication as well. We were capturing these stories on video. Set up a video camera and people just freeze up. It takes a while to thaw them. So the interviews I planned were rather stiff. Oh every once in awhile one of the tax preparers would forget that the camera was running and he or she would start to tell stories. Nothing earth shattering. Just a nice tale of wanting to do a good job for the client.

I've done a lot of these types of interviews, and the most valuable lesson I've learned over time is that the best stories happen after the interview ends. I've made it a practice to leave the camera running after formally announcing the end of the interview. It's amazing to watch interviewees' demeanor change when I say that the interview has come to an end. They relax and laugh. I can understand why. It's stressful if you don't spend much time in front of a camera.

People do really like to talk about who they are and what they do. Just not on camera. So after I announced that the interview was over, I asked each tax preparer, "Why do you do this?" I wasn't prepared for what happened. That one question unleashed a flood of stories.

One person told me of the incredible sense of responsibility she felt. She explained that, once a year, her clients lay out their entire financial life in front of her. People are notoriously insecure and tight-lipped about their finances. And they showed her more about their lives than they showed their closest family. This was an incredibly vulnerable moment for them. And she took it as a monumental sign of trust. That made her so proud. She felt like a trusted part of those people's lives. As she told me this, tears welled up. She just couldn't help it.

Another tax preparer told me how clients would enter the office worried and stressed. By the time they were finished, they were physically changed. He said that it was incredibly gratifying to see the relief on their faces. He had never had a job that made him feel like he was doing something so worthwhile.

Were these tax preparers living the mission? Honestly, they couldn't tell you what the mission was. But they were acting on something. They had a palpable sense of purpose. They knew that they could make a profound difference in people's lives. And that ignited them. As Ian Percy says, "You don't just have a purpose, the purpose has you."[14]

They told story after story. This is what got them out of bed in the morning. It was what sustained them through the long days of tax season. It wasn't a corporate mission. It was a purpose. A purpose they considered very personal. If you stopped and thought about it, I'd bet you'd be able to easily recall your own stories of the things that have ignited your passion. Things that energized your efforts, making work feel less like work and more like a vocation. I'd also bet those things felt very personal.

This is a powerful lesson for all of us. If we want to get people engaged, it can't just be about business. We have to give people something that connects with them in a meaningful way. And on an individual level. It's got to get personal.

Why do we leave our passion behind when we go to work?

"To wear your heart on your sleeve." It means to make your feelings apparent. That should be a good thing, right? Yet when the phrase is used, it connotes a weakness in the person you are describing.

"Sue really wears her heart on her sleeve."

Why is that? In this age of radical transparency making your feelings known would seem to be a desirable trait.

That aside, wouldn't it be awesome to know someone's passions? I'm not talking about hobbies (I don't mean to squelch your enthusiasm for your interpretive dance class or the amateur taxidermy you do.) I'm talking about causes and movements that could make our world a little bit better place to live.

Think about the times we've heard anybody speak passionately about something he or she believed in. It's infectious, right? We can't help but feel at least a little exhilaration if they are genuinely excited.

Shouldn't that be encouraged?

Having passion is generally considered to be a good thing. Right up to the point you walk through the door of your place of work. In general, the majority of businesses are not oriented to tap into a collective passion of the people who work there.

Managers will tell you they want workers to have a passion. But it's a passion for error-free spreadsheets and making sure the TPS reports are turned in on time (with a cover sheet included.) But that's more diligence than it is passion.

It's hard to blame them. Having a purpose that drives passion doesn't usually start as a grassroots movement. So in its absence, workers simply punch in and punch out. Managers manage the metrics that they are being held accountable for hitting. We all sigh and say, "Well, that's just how it is." But is it?

What if everyone felt so strongly about the organization's purpose that they let their passion show? What if we collectively wore our hearts on our sleeves? What would happen? According to a post from Fast Company, "Purpose people are more engaged, more productive, better champions of the company, and tend to stay longer in their roles, according to the surveys. So companies should look to hire purpose-oriented people when they can, and promote them where possible."[15]

Think about what that would be like. All these people showing up to work everyday and feeling confident – and even encouraged – about letting their passion show for the work they were doing.

Knowing that the work was making a difference. Imagine how that could accelerate a business.

Organizations bring in efficiency experts. They launch employee motivation programs. Yet most miss the one thing that has the power to unlock untold potential. It's embracing a Big Audacious Meaning.

We'll go out of our way to help others through a cause that is near and dear to us. We'll volunteer. We'll give money. We'll even put aside personal wants in order to help. Why is that? Because these things help us feel a sense of purpose.

Yet, for the vast majority of us, that kind of energy and enthusiasm gets left behind when we head off to our jobs. We spend half our waking hours at work. Half! Why are we so willing to allow half our time to be so uninspiring?

In his classic *Working*, Studs Terkle said, "Work is about a search for daily meaning as well as daily bread, for recognition as well as cash, for astonishment rather than torpor; in short, for a sort of life rather than a Monday through Friday sort of dying."[16]

Those last 7 words are like a punch in the gut. I find myself immediately asking, "Am I pursuing a purpose, or have I just accepted 'a Monday through Friday sort of dying'?"

We can say that there is nothing we can do. That the organization or the culture is too impenetrable. That's understandable. It's not true. But it's understandable. Sometimes it's just easier to punch the clock and collect the paycheck.

Until we read those last 7 words again.

People are yearning for purpose. And if we give it to them, we may just be surprised how proudly they wear it. Right there on their sleeves.

"Who cares?"

Consider the question, "Who cares?" Are we really inquiring about whom in the general vicinity may have an emotional attachment? No. It has actually become less of a question and more of an indictment of a lack of emotional resonance. We're not looking for an answer when we utter, "Who cares?" We use it to point out that an idea, a feature, a process, etc. has very little merit.

Here's the fascinating part. We use the word 'care'. We don't say, "Who has an interest?" Interest is rational. To make our point, we get straight to the emotional. We ask, "Who *cares*?"

We want life to have meaning. We want to feel like the hours we spend and the effort we put forth each day have a positive impact in the world we live in. This is why we align with causes that match our belief system.

It's why we put bumper stickers on our cars and wear slogans on our t-shirts. It's why we donate and volunteer. We yearn to care. Yet so many brands miss this about us. The ones that do get it get our attention.

Jim Collins and Jerry Porras emphasize this need, "People still have a fundamental human need to belong to something they can feel proud of. They have a fundamental need for guiding values and sense of purpose that gives their life and work meaning."[17]

What if we actually asked the question as a touchstone for our organization? Right now, the question/statement means, "No one cares." What if we took it literally? What if we used it to discover the compelling reasons a specific type of person would form an emotional bond with our organization? Suddenly, it becomes much, much more than a demeaning snipe. It becomes a challenge for all of us to find the emotional clout that can give people that much sought after reason to care.

Because nobody is motivated by mediocre meaning

Nobody jumps out of bed in the morning thinking, "I can't wait to get to work and spread a little more mediocrity in the world!" We all want to feel like we are contributing. And we get really stoked when we feel like what we are doing is making the world a little better place.

When we have that kind of motivation, we work a little harder. We dream up and create unexpected solutions. Because at that point, it's not just about you or me. It's about us. And the difference we are making for others.

In my firm's financial services practice area, I wrote this manifesto to explain to prospects the meaningful and worthwhile purpose behind our efforts:

We do what we do in financial services marketing for one very simple reason. We believe that no one should have to feel intimidated by money.

We believe our financial lives should be easier to understand. Our money and information should be accessible, when and where we choose. And it should all help us feel more in control, so we feel like we can make good decisions.

We are on a mission to help create this invaluable confidence. Confidence that can change the course of a life. Because none of us should have to feel intimidated by something we work so hard to get.

Money can be a wonderful thing. But we also know it is the cause of a myriad of problems – from health issues to divorce. We wanted to do something about that.

Every time I have stood up and recited this manifesto to prospects good things have happened. People love the purpose. It gets them thinking about their own brand and the Big Audacious Meaning that they could embrace.

What we care about is not rational

Psychologist Daniel Kahneman describes it this way, "We think, each of us, that we're much more rational than we are. And we think that we make our decisions because we have good reasons to make them. Even when it's the other way around. We believe in the reasons, because we've already made the decision."[18]

Duke University Professor of Psychology and Behavioral Economics Dan Ariely illustrates this with a great story.

He tells of using an online tool to decide which car was right for him. He answered a battery of questions only to discover that the car that matched him and his needs was a nondescript midsize sedan.

So did this man of science accept, without emotion, the rational outcome? Of course not. He's human. He did what any of us would do. He went back and changed the answers until he got to that result that he felt like was the car that was right for him. For Ariely, it was a sporty roadster. Ariely tells this story to help us understand that we all are irrational decision makers.[19]

University of Southern California Neuroscience professor Antonio Damasio said it perhaps most eloquently, "We are not thinking machines; we are feeling machines that think." His research and studies in neuroscience continue to reveal the surprisingly dominant role that our emotions play.[20]

Key Takeaways

- If we want to get people engaged, it can't just be about business. We have to give people something that connects with them on an individual level. It's got to get personal.

- Organizations bring in efficiency experts. They launch employee motivation programs. Yet most miss the one thing that has the power to unlock untold potential. It's embracing a Big Audacious Meaning.

- We'll go out of our way to help others through a cause that is near and dear to us. We'll volunteer. We'll give money. We'll even put aside personal wants in order to help. Why is that? Because these things help us feel a sense of purpose.

- We want life to have meaning. We want to feel like the hours we spend and the effort we put forth each day has a positive impact in the world we live in. This is why we align with causes that match our belief system.

- We don't say, "Who has an interest?" Interest is rational. To make our point, we get straight to the emotional. We ask, "Who cares?"

- Right now asking "Who cares?" means "No one cares." What if we took it literally? What if we used it to discover the compelling reasons a specific type of person would form an emotional bond with our organization? Suddenly, it becomes a challenge for all of us to find the emotional clout that can give people that much sought after reason to care.

- We all are emotional decision makers. No matter how rational we may think we are.

SECTION 3: WHY IT'S SMART FOR AN ORGANIZATION

Having a Big Audacious Meaning is a good and noble thing. But it is also a business strategy. It can be deployed to do everything from boost new client acquisition to increase employee engagement.

Now, there is a fine line here. If you read this and say, "We need to use this purpose thing." Well, we have a problem. Purpose is not a gimmick. Treating it as such is manipulative. If that admonishment is not enough, then know this: if we use it in this way, it will backfire - leaving us with reputation damage that will have us wishing that we never heard of this concept of a Big Audacious Meaning. The world is too connected today. People can out your insincerity with lightning speed. And then share your attempted manipulations with the world. Nothing spreads faster than the hint that some corporation is trying to game our emotions for their gain.

Here is the interesting dichotomy. This connectivity and transparency that can strike a fatal blow to our brand reputation are the very same means that can rocket the positive perception of our brand into the stratosphere.

If we are really serving a higher purpose, people will reward us for it. Yes, I'm talking about heightened brand perception. But also monetary rewards. Studies show that consumers reward brands that are driven by purpose.[21] And we haven't even addressed all the magic it creates for employee retention and recruiting. Which brings us back to that crucial point. Purpose is a business strategy. When delivered honestly and with transparency, it can transform a business.

Purpose is easily thought of as doing good. But what often gets lost is that it's just as much about doing well.

CHAPTER 6
The value of meaning

A Big Audacious Meaning can energize an organization, fueling growth and success. In some ways, it's very logical. Team members, customers, and prospects are emboldened. They are engaged. And they are inspired. Good things happen when you create that kind of environment with your organization.

According to a survey from Deloitte, "91% of respondents (executives and employees) who said their company had a strong sense of purpose also said their company had a history of strong financial performance."[22]

A Big Audacious Meaning will drive growth. More importantly, it results in high quality growth. It gives our prospects an incredibly powerful reason to engage. So we can reduce our reliance on discounts, gimmicks, and giveaways – all things that drive short-term success, but also train our prospects to wait to engage until they're given some sort of deal.

As Roy Spence explains, "The more purpose driven you actually are -- in other words, the more people who believe in what you stand for and relate to your values -- the less spending you have to do to convince people of your value."[23]

A Big Audacious Meaning also helps us sustain growth. If it's just about the price, then customers will evaporate the next time somebody else comes along with a little bit better deal. With a Big Audacious Meaning, any growth we generate will have a higher likelihood of sustaining. Because we're aligning with our prospects beliefs and not simply with their need to find the best deal. That helps generate impressive results for an organization.

Harvard professors John Kotter and James Heskett illustrate the impact in their book *Corporate Culture and Performance*. They report that firms with shared-values–based cultures enjoyed 400% higher revenues, 700% greater job growth, 1,200% higher stock prices and significantly faster profit performance, as compared to companies in similar industries.[24]

Marketing professor Rajendra Sisodia and his coauthors add more evidence in their book *Firms of Endearment* by highlighting how companies that put employees' and customers' needs ahead of shareholders' desires outperform conventional competitors in stock-market performance by 8:1.[25]

A Big Audacious Meaning supercharges an organization by creating an irresistible story and a call for all our prospects to become part of that story. This creates unparalleled desire for and loyalty to the brand. This is significant because a brand can be one of the most valuable business assets we create. In fact, powerful brands have accounted for anywhere from 30% to 60% of the valuation of their companies. "Accenture determined that intangible assets account for about 70% of the value of the S&P 500, up from 20% in 1980."[26]

Customers love meaningful brands. In fact, they will more willingly engage with these brands. And will even pay more for a brand because of its ability to align with what they consider meaningful and important. This point is punctuated by a post from Forbes.com that states, "Ninety one percent of consumers would switch brands if a different one of similar price and quality supported a good cause."[27]

The value of creating caring

We are in an era where much energy is spent deploying technologies in order to advance a business. We look at how we can automate functions. We look at how we can capture and analyze data to make better decisions. These are all valuable and worthwhile endeavors. But the technology is not enough. At some point, we have to help our prospects care.

Technology was at play when society shifted from the craftsman to mass manufacturing. We don't have to look any further than Henry Ford to see a great example. The assembly line was a technological advancement that gave him a business advantage. But it wasn't too much later that competitors had adopted the advancement, and all the car manufacturers realized they needed something beyond the process to continue to build an advantage. They turned to the creativity of branding to tap into the powerful emotional drivers that created customer preference.

In this new era of branding, the car became more than just a machine to get us from point A to point B. The car became a reflection of who we were. It symbolized everything from our economic status to our personality. And it came to represent a sense of freedom. The ability to conquer distances.

New technological advancements will always offer a functional advantage. But technology will always commoditize as well. It is happening at an ever-accelerating pace. Just as the car companies experienced, we will need something more than just connecting with the functional needs of prospects. We will need to understand how to tap into their aspirations. That is even more reason to understand the power of a Big Audacious Meaning.

People are going to make decisions with their emotions.

Even after going through a very rational process. We are all wired this way. Telling the world what you do is a rational approach. It appeals to the neocortex or the portion of the brain responsible for analytic thought and language. For example, a rational message for a bank is, "We help people manage their money through checking, savings, and lending."

Telling the world why you do what you do is an emotional approach. It appeals to the limbic region – it is the portion of the brain responsible for feeling and decision-making. An emotional message for a bank is, "We make it simple for people to have more control over their money so they can capture that elusive confidence that gives them the power to pursue those things that they've always wanted to do but didn't think they could."

The emotional message allows us to connect with the larger purpose behind our efforts. And in return, pack more of a wallop. Great brands understand this and deliver an emotional message to prospects and customers.

According to the Disney Institute, organizations that optimize the emotional connection with prospects outperform competitors by 26% in gross margin and 85% in sales growth.[28]

The Disney Institute report went on to state that, emotionally engaged customers are at least three times more likely to recommend, three times more likely to re-purchase, less likely to shop around, and much less price sensitive.

The Vulcan argument

In the TV series *Star Trek*, Vulcans were emotionless, rational thinkers. Through the years, I've run into clients who gave me what I call the Vulcan argument. It goes like this, "This is a totally rational and logical decision for our prospects. We don't need to worry about purpose and meaning, we just need to give them the facts."

They usually explain that it's because we're talking to technically-oriented people such as engineers or financial analysts. As if being technically oriented makes you less human.

Being an engineer or a financial analyst is *what* someone does. But being human is *who* we are. It is our biology. It is not something that we can simply choose to ignore.

Because we are human, we are powerfully affected by the meaning conveyed through stories. Especially when a Big Audacious Meaning powers those stories.

Yet, every time we feel it necessary to make a case, we default to the numbers. It happens when we want to justify what we did or even what we want to do.

"Let me show you the research numbers on this. I have a scatter chart that will blow you away!"

And by 'blow away' we usually mean that you may nod approvingly, but if asked 15 minutes later to repeat those numbers, you'd do what most of us do. Scratch our heads and say something like, "I don't remember it exactly, but I think it was pretty good?"

Chip Heath demonstrated this in his "Making Ideas Stick" class at Stanford University. He had his students participate in an exercise that involved giving and listening to speeches on a potentially emotional issue. The result of the exercise was telling. "When students are asked to recall speeches, 63 percent remember the stories. Only 5 percent remember any individual statistic."[29]

I don't expect you to remember that stat. Only that stories are more memorable than numbers. It's just how we're wired. In fact, anybody who can seem to remember detailed statistics is either lying or trying to sell us something. Or both.

The more interesting fact from that finding above was that a majority of the students remembered the stories.

In my work with Water.org, I saw this phenomenon come to life in a simple example. Water.org has some startling statistics about the global water crisis. For example, 2.3 billion people around the world lack access to a toilet. That's billions with a 'b'. That is a blow-you-away statistic. Except, when people would try to repeat that statistic from memory, they could never quite get the number right. For the most part, they'd remember it was in the billions, but there were lots of errors with the real number. And honestly, the point kind of lost its impact as the one delivering the fact fumbled with the statistic.

The funny thing is that they could tell you without hesitation that more people have access to a cell phone than a toilet.

See what just happened there? Turn the statistic into a story and suddenly you have something that is memorable. Something that is humanly relatable. And, ultimately, irresistibly shareable. Because stories are human. And we humans like things that are, well, human.

The availability of data gets a lot of attention in today's world. It's incredibly important. But its full potential can never be realized unless we transform those numbers into stories. I have some data in a PowerPoint that proves it. But I'd rather just tell you a story about it.

Key Takeaways

- A Big Audacious Meaning will drive high quality growth, reducing our reliance on discounts, gimmicks, and giveaways. Furthermore, it's sustainable growth.

- A Big Audacious Meaning creates unparalleled desire for and loyalty to the brand – one of the most valuable business assets we create.

- Customers will more willingly engage with purpose-driven brands and even pay more because of the brand's ability to align with what they consider meaningful and important.

- New technological advancements can offer a functional advantage, but technology will always commoditize. To have a sustainable advantage, we will need to understand how to tap into our prospects' aspirations.

- Telling the world what you do is a rational approach. It appeals to the neocortex or the portion of the brain responsible for analytic thought and language. Telling the world why you do what you do is an emotional approach. It appeals to the limbic region – the portion of the brain responsible for feeling and decision-making.

- According to the Disney Institute, organizations that optimize the emotional connection outperform competitors, build loyalty, and get recommended.

- Because we are human, we are powerfully affected by the meaning conveyed through stories. Especially when a Big Audacious Meaning powers those stories.

CHAPTER 7
Shifting to prosperity

First things first. Let's stop portraying 'profit' as a dirty word. It's ludicrous to hear people denounce companies by saying, "They're just trying to make a profit." Of course they are. Ideally, a company operates well and generates a profit. It then uses that profit to reinvest to continue to advance. That reinvestment has the potential to benefit the company, the employees, and the community. It's a good theory. One that has even been proven to work in the past. Yet somewhere along the way, things got out of whack. Economist William Lazonick gives us an insightful explanation in a Harvard Business Review article:

"From the end of World War II until the late 1970s, a retain-and-reinvest approach to resource allocation prevailed at major U.S. corporations. They retained earnings and reinvested them in increasing their capabilities, first and foremost in the employees who helped make firms more competitive. They provided workers with higher incomes and greater job security, thus contributing to equitable, stable economic growth—what I call "sustainable prosperity".

This pattern began to break down in the late 1970s, giving way to a downsize-and-distribute regime of reducing costs and then distributing the freed-up cash to financial interests, particularly shareholders. By favoring value extraction over value creation, this approach has contributed to employment instability and income inequality."[30]

This could explain stagnant wage growth, lack of employee

loyalty, and a whole litany of challenges facing the world of work. The most confounding thing about this is how shortsighted it is. If the average Joe doesn't participate in the spoils of this success, then he eventually pulls back his spending. We live in an economy that relies on the ability of us all to spend. If we don't spend, then the companies suffer. And there's even less of a chance for those organizations to share any profit. It's a downward spiral. But if companies focus on prosperity, then everyone shares in the gains. Which means people can spend and companies can do well.

The point is that profit is not the problem. It's what the organization chooses to do with that profit.

We need to switch out profit for prosperity.

Profit is an inward focus. Profit is something we generate by how we manage all the variables associated with our offering. It minimizes the role of stakeholders outside the company. Oh, we may refer to them as "partners", but it really is not much more than them being a partner in helping us achieve our profit goals.

Prosperity, on the other hand, is how we all benefit together. It goes back to the old cliché, "A rising tide lifts all boats." This is not a call to abandon capitalism. This is very much about the business doing well. But it is rooted in the idea that a business can do well by doing good.

Our believers purchase from us to receive the goods and services and all the benefits, but there can be something more. There can be the feeling that they are contributing to the Big Audacious Meaning the brand has embraced. In purchasing, they become collaborators in helping work toward the real and meaningful impact the brand will have for everyone. In other words, the prosperity of us all.

In his book, *The Story of Purpose: The Path to Creating a Brighter Brand, a Greater Company, and a Lasting Legacy*, Joey Reiman muses, "Perhaps we got the idea of business wrong in the first place. It was not to transact but to transform."[31]

The brand can become the catalyst for prosperity. And we all can become more than fans. We can become that special breed that invests both its dollars and its passion. We can become collaborators in creating prosperity for all of those around us.

Protecting ourselves from ourselves

A focus on prosperity begins with clarifying and pursuing our Big Audacious Meaning. A Big Audacious Meaning is built on a commitment to serving those around us to make a difference in a life, a community, or even the world. Our primary focus isn't on ourselves. We are driven by the needs of those we serve. And we believe our profitability is tied to helping make a difference for those around us.

The reason this works is because it protects us from us. How many times have we seen or heard of organizations making questionable decisions because of a myopic, profit-at-all-costs focus. When we are pursuing a Big Audacious Meaning, we prime everyone to be making better decisions. Because we are all focused on prosperity as the desired outcome - not just profitability.

In his book, *Drive: The Surprising Truth About What Motivates Us*, Daniel Pink gives this explanation, "We're learning that the profit motive, potent though it is, can be an insufficient impetus for both individuals and organizations. An equally powerful source of energy, one we've often neglected or dismissed as unrealistic, is what we might call the "purpose motive." Many entrepreneurs, executives, and investors are realizing that the best performing companies stand for something and contribute to the world."[32]

It would be easy to dismiss this as a naive notion. To characterize it as nothing more than wishful thinking. Except, there are organizations that have embraced prosperity. And you know what? They're profitable. In fact, they outperform their peers.

Let's change what "good business" means

It's a funny thing when people say, "It's just good business." They don't mean it's the most optimal thing to do for the business. More often than not, it means the numbers are in the right rows. The columns add up.

Being fiscally responsible is critically important. But too often, we miss exploring the full potential of what we could accomplish by hiding behind this excuse of fiscal responsibility.

The danger here is that this type of "It's just good business" thinking pretty much guarantees adequate results.

Is that what we really want to be? Adequate?

Don't answer that. Consider this first. By limiting ourselves, we may actually be exposing our business to more risk than what we were originally trying to avoid!

That doesn't even sound adequate.

We need sound and rational decisions. Otherwise we'll end up with another situation like the dot com bust at the turn of the century. We need responsible practices. It's just that "good business" holds the potential to help us do so much more.

Imagine not only adhering to responsible business practices, but also embracing a larger purpose. Imagine a well-run business that also helps make a difference in lives, a community, or even the world. Companies like Kind and Warby Parker are proving that this is a business acceleration strategy. The genius is that they realize this isn't a zero-sum game. They realize they can create good and create profit at the same time.

Dove is another great example. It would have been easy for the beauty brand to dismiss this calling by protesting, "We're just a manufacturer." But there was a belief that what they manufactured could have bigger ramifications. A belief that their impact was larger than just leaving skin clean, soft, and smooth. A belief that they could help all women raise their self-esteem and realize their full potential.

Dove adopted this idea and saw the impact it could have (both financially and socially) because they believed in something bigger than their product's attributes. And by the way, Dove could have hung their appeal on the fact that they are "...the #1 Dermatologist Recommended brand in the US, Canada and France and strongly endorsed by Dermatologists across the world."[33] It's an important fact. But they believed that their story could embrace something bigger.

In 2004, Dove commissioned a study called, *The Real Truth About Beauty: A Global Report*. The study looked to investigate, "...a growing concern that portrayals of female beauty in popular culture were helping to perpetuate an idea of beauty that was neither authentic nor attainable."[34]

The report uncovered that only 2% of women around the world would describe themselves as beautiful.

This is significant when you consider that self-image can have a huge impact on the lives of women everywhere, affecting everything from health to financial success. Driven by the findings, Dove launched The Campaign For Real Beauty.

Dove could have put its focus on how its products help women take care of themselves, and as a result, help them have a little more confidence. That would have been an honorable focus that would have helped make a difference in individual lives.

But the Big Audacious Meaning reached beyond that. Dove didn't just want women to change the soap that they used. The organization wanted the world to change the way it talked about and even defined beauty.

Dove continues to sponsor research that uncovers important findings. For example, the brand revealed that, "72% of girls feel tremendous pressure to be beautiful."[35]

The brand uses these findings to inspire their advertising, championing the idea that we all need to change our paradigm about beauty.

It even went so far as to create the Dove Self-Esteem Fund to inspire and educate girls and women about a wider definition of beauty.

Could our brand aspire to something more like Dove did? Before we dismiss the idea, imagine someone asking, "Could a soap maker change how we define beauty and in the process help improve the self-esteem of women around the world?"

The prosperity movement has begun. Are you on board?

In his book, *The Purpose Economy: How Your Desire for Impact, Personal Growth and Community Is Changing the World*, Aaron Hurst highlights the growth of the movement, "Among other measures, CEOs expect demand for purpose in the consumer marketplace to increase by nearly 300 percent by 2020."[36]

This is a shift from the old school practices that separated the profit-focused mechanisms of an organization from its social responsibility efforts. The old way of thinking saw these as two separate and largely unrelated parts of the company. Their connection was loose at best.

The new movement is demonstrating that optimizing growth depends on optimizing purpose. And, renowned organizations have begun to build research behind the practice.

Harvard Business Review continues to generate thought leadership about purpose in business today. Harvard Business Review Analytic Service published The Business Case for Purpose - a study that looks at why and how companies are embracing purpose to inform organizational transformation.[37]

Additionally, the University of Oxford Saïd Business School has been releasing a series of reports covering how organizations are using purpose to address their challenges around transformation and growth.[38]

Organizations of all types are looking for ways to build a sustainable path to success in a world where technology and connectivity drive rapid change. It's no wonder that the idea of purpose is becoming the keystone of business strategy for forward-thinking organizations.

In the shifting sands of the current environment, organizations of all types are starting to see how purpose can provide the solid footing that allows them to confidently push forward. A footing built from the belief that meaning and money go hand-in-hand. That by doing good, they will do well.

Key Takeaways

- Ideally, a company operates well and generates a profit. It then uses that profit to reinvest to benefit the company, the employees, and the community. Somewhere along the way, things got out of whack.

- If companies focus on prosperity, then everyone shares in the gains. Which means people can spend and companies can do well.

- In purchasing, our prospects become collaborators in helping work toward the Big Audacious Meaning the brand embraces. In other words, the prosperity of us all.

- A focus on prosperity begins with clarifying and pursuing our Big Audacious Meaning. It is rooted in the idea that our success is tied to helping make a difference for those around us.

- When we are pursuing a Big Audacious Meaning, we prime everyone to be making better decisions. Because we are all focused on prosperity as the desired outcome - not just profitability.

- Companies like Kind, Warby Parker, and Dove are proving that this is a business acceleration strategy.

- The new movement is demonstrating that optimizing growth depends on optimizing purpose. And, renowned organizations have begun to build research behind the belief that meaning and money go hand-in-hand. That by doing good, we will do well.

SECTION 4: CLARIFYING THE BIG AUDACIOUS MEANING

Not everyone is at the same stage of what I'll call purpose maturity. At one end of the spectrum are organizations that have begun to articulate their purpose and put it into action. At the other end are those that value a purpose, but are just beginning to explore the idea.

No matter where an organization is, there is something we can be doing to help make the most of that desire to capture both purpose and profit. To make money and meaning. Here's a simple breakdown of 3 stages of purpose maturity and what to do at each stage.

Stage 1 - Discover

Organizations at this stage are just beginning to understand what a Big Audacious Meaning can do for them. They are looking to define it, establish how it could come to life throughout the organization, and spread out into the world. A thoughtful discovery can provide the foundation. It can reveal the drivers of purpose and help provide the guiding principles that will inform the collaborations where the Big Audacious Meaning will emerge.

Stage 2 - Clarify

Some organizations have a sense of purpose, but have either never clarified it or need to redefine it. In some instances, they may be trying to use their mission statement as a way to express it (a mission statement simply cannot capture what a purpose or Big Audacious Meaning delivers.) It's critical to go through a process of clarifying the Big Audacious Meaning in order to arrive at a focused and well-articulated purpose. Additionally, there may be some confusion around what an organization believes, what it is currently doing (corporate social responsibility, volunteering, etc.) and how it brings it all together to make all the efforts more powerful. This calls for an investigation process to identify where there may be a disconnect or to uncover opportunity. The investigation is a vital part of the process within both Stages 2 & 3.

Stage 3 - Confirm

Organizations at this stage have identified a purpose and may have even begun to introduce it throughout the organization. Sparked by a sense that there is potential left untapped, leaders at this stage will ask, "Are we doing everything we can to take full advantage of our purpose?" At this point, it's important to go through a process of confirming the Big Audacious Meaning to ensure there is a unifying definition that is accepted universally through the organization. This should be coupled with an investigation (as described at Stage 2) to determine where there are opportunities for the purpose to elevate the business.

We can't assume that everyone we hope to serve knows our Big Audacious Meaning. Vagueness saps its power. Uncertainty will leave awesome opportunities unexplored. We need to find the clarity. And we need to be measured in our efforts to bring it to all our stakeholders. Because when our Big Audacious Meaning is clear, so is our future.

CHAPTER 8
Setting the stage

The quest to find our Big Audacious Meaning can be one of the most gratifying experiences that we undertake. There is something that feels honorable about pursuing that thing that will lead to our organization defining how it will make a profound difference in a life, a community, or even the world.

There will be work involved. There always is with anything worthwhile. But there is something different between the toil and labor that the mundane tasks of the day demand and this search for purpose. I almost hate to use the word 'work' to define the quest. This is different. It should be exhilarating. It should ignite a passion among our team. And when that a-ha moment arrives, it should be accompanied by a profound sense of accomplishment.

Planning for buy-in

At some point, we will want to introduce our Big Audacious Meaning to the entire organization. We will have gone through some great work to clarify our purpose. There will be heated debate. There will be passionate lobbying. And there will be that revelatory moment when our Big Audacious Meaning emerges.

We will be anxious to tell everyone. We will be passionate. We will be excited. We'll set it up with pomp and circumstance. And we'll reveal it with a flourish. And then it happens. Crickets.

Our people won't understand what it all means. They may nod along and clap politely. It's easy to be crestfallen. How could they not see the world-shaking implications of this? The answer is obvious when we step back. They haven't been on the journey with us. They will come along eventually. Once they have been exposed to the new thinking enough times and they have had the opportunity to connect the dots.

But that's not what we were hoping for. And it could have been avoided.

This is why we need to think about buy-in before we begin any of this. This can be tough. It's easy to get everyone involved once we have a program defined. But as we're beginning the process, it's too easy for the management team to take a command and control attitude. After all, we're talking about a discovery. It can be messy. We're going to get input that we may not agree with. But if we don't build the inclusion from the beginning, we're just increasing the amount of time it will take for our Big Audacious Meaning to really take hold in the organization. On the other hand, if we invite the organization in and embrace this controlled chaos, we can build engagement that takes root and flourishes quickly.

I have conducted discoveries that bring together groups of stakeholders from every corner of the organization. The advantage of this is that a large number of team members feel like they are part of the evolution. They have buy in. So when that moment of the big reveal comes, we have a genuinely fervent group cheering the Big Audacious Meaning. I've been at these events. I've seen people wiping away tears and standing and cheering. Because they understand. They have had a passion ignited and it has come to a zenith.

I've had some organizations that couldn't pull these kinds of groups together. In these cases, we need two things to happen. First, we need to have representatives that cover all parts of the organization and who are well regarded. That latter part is extremely important. These are the people that can help us build adoption. And second, we need them to report on the progress throughout the process and even solicit feedback that they can bring back to the stakeholder group in charge of the discovery. Again, the goal is to make everyone feel like they have a say in the fate of their everyday work life. If we do this, we'll create a group of true believers that will help us do some amazing things.

The dormant army of evangelists right under our nose

What happens when a purpose gets handed off to the uninitiated? Here's what I mean. A leadership team goes through the process of clarifying a compelling purpose. They declare how it will make a profound difference in a life, a community, or even the world.

All those involved agree that this is momentous. There is an incomparable feeling of accomplishment and hope for the future.

Then the purpose is handed off to the next level of management. A group who has no ownership stake in its creation. Yet, they are charged with bringing that purpose to life in everything that the organization says and does.

Immediate disaster? No. More like a slow, torturous sucking of the soul.

"We need to tone down the personality."

I've actually heard this said from that next level of management as we began to express the purpose. Here's the really sad part: it's happened more than once.

If this brand were a person (which is a great way to think about a brand) would we want someone who has "toned down the personality"? Just like when I meet people. I don't much care for those passionate and engaging people. Give me someone who is noncommittal and forgettable. Just like this guy I met the other day. What was his name? Give me a minute. It will come to me.

Nope. I got nothing.

It's hard to blame that next level of management. They weren't engaged from the get go. They haven't been inspired by the incredible vision of the profound impact the brand could have on its believers.

With no inspiration and no bold ideals, they do what they have always done. They return to the safe harbor of corporate speak and middle-of-the-road blandness that is easy for committees to approve.

Our team members are the most powerful set of believers we will have. When they truly embrace our purpose, things will accelerate.

So before we begin the process, let's engage them. And I mean really engage them. Accept the fact that they may add a point of view that we hadn't anticipated. Let's not squelch it. They will know if we're just paying lip service to their ideas (that's a guaranteed way of ensuring our efforts never take off).

Whoops. We didn't engage our team members before starting. That's not ideal, but it doesn't mean we need to throw out everything and start over. It does mean going back to our team members (or creating that team member stakeholder group). We must be prepared. They may add some things that will mean making some changes. It's well worth it. We will reap the benefit in the momentum that we will feel when we roll out the new brand purpose.

The great thing about a Big Audacious Meaning is that it is infectious. When done well, it's brimming with meaning for everyone who has been included. It's virtually impossible to contain it. Everyone connected to it will want to share it. Because it gives meaning to our days. It declares how we will make a profound difference for our fellow human beings. Imagine having a stake in the emergence of that. Imagine feeling ownership in something that powerful. As opposed to being handed something that you didn't help form and being told to make it come to life.

Selecting and preparing our stakeholders

There are a few things we need to do before we jump into our workshop session. These include identifying our workshop participants or core stakeholders, prepping them for the task ahead, and gathering input that will ensure the fruitfulness of the workshop.

First, let's talk about our core stakeholders. This is not a job for the disinterested or even the mildly engaged. Most importantly, beware the cynics. Let's face it. The world is full of them. Being a cynic is easy. You don't have to make an emotional commitment. You don't have to put yourself out there. You can wear your snarky detachment like a badge.

Don't mistake pointed criticism from the coolly detached as enlightened insight. Instead, look for committed thoughtfulness. We'll find it among those willing to put their passion out there. It may be in bold ways. It may be in quiet ways. If we are to harness the full power of the Big Audacious Meaning, we need these fearless, passionately committed folks.

They must be considered leaders. Not just because they have the title. They must be respected by their peers and have the ability to carry a brave, new idea deep into the organization. This is our purpose dream team. Choose them wisely. No fewer than five. No more than twelve.

Jim Collins and Jerry Porras give this guidance, "…in many situations we like to suggest a "Mars Group." It works like this: Imagine you've been asked to recreate the very best attributes of your organization on another planet, but you only have seats on the rocket ship for five to seven people. Who would you send? They are the people who likely have a gut-level understanding of your core values, have the highest level of credibility with their peers, and the highest level of competence. We'll often ask a group of people brought together to work on core values to nominate a Mars Group of five to seven individuals."[39]

Choosing the right core stakeholders is one of the most crucial steps we can take to ensure something inspiring and magical happening. And then sustaining the magic as we roll out the Big Audacious Meaning to team members, customers, prospects, and the world.

Next, it is critical that all those involved understand the objectives of the process and the invaluable outcomes. Hopefully, they are all equally excited about embarking on the journey, but it's not unusual that there will be a few that grudgingly show up and participate at the absolute minimum level. This can be overcome. There are ways to engage these folks during the process. But if one of these is the CEO, President, or other top person, it can suck the enthusiasm out of the room and reduce the whole effort to average at best.

The problem isn't that these curmudgeons are impossible to engage. Most often, they haven't been properly prepped for what is about to happen. We do this by setting expectations before the process begins.

Setting expectations covers the questions that every person has. We can't assume that everyone has worked through these for themselves. We can't assume that the reasons and rationales are obvious. In fact, we can't assume anything. We need to build understanding and manage expectations. There are three things that make this happen.

- **Help them understand what is involved** - it may seem obvious to us, but let's put ourselves in their shoes. We are pulling them away from their responsibilities and asking for their intense focus on something that they may not yet understand in the way that we do. It would be a rare person who could come into a workshop with just a cursory knowledge of what will transpire and just give themselves over to the process. The more likely scenario is that a person will be hesitant and guarded. That's not the posture we want for something as important as what we are undertaking.

- **Help them understand what will be required of everyone** - they will have questions. They may not get voiced, but the questions will be there. Things like, "What will I be required to do?" And, "Will I be required to do things that will make me feel uncomfortable?" If they understand what will be asked of them, we will have an easier time engaging them and drawing out their insights.

- **Help them understand what will be accomplished** – let's paint the picture of what they will be a part of. And help them feel the benefit of fully engaging. People like being part of something meaningful. Big and meaningful is even better. Let's help them see how committing their passion can result in great things.

We have to look at our stakeholders as our audience and promote this to them just as we would promote an idea to our most valuable prospects. Deliver succinct and well-designed materials to them first. This allows them to engage with the information on their own schedule. I would also hold a short kickoff meeting (this can be a webinar) where we walk through all the information that answers the questions we outlined. This allows them to passively absorb the information (especially if they haven't dedicated the time to look through the materials we sent). Finally, spark their imagination. Help them understand what we can accomplish. Use examples of other organizations that have committed to discovering and defining a Big Audacious Meaning. Use rational evidence like the gain in market share it has helped others capture. Then wrap it in compelling photos and video to show how that Big Audacious Meaning came to life for them. Help them understand that they have the opportunity to be part of something equally as compelling and profound.

Key Takeaways

- If we don't build buy-in throughout the organization from the beginning, we're just increasing the amount of time it will take for our Big Audacious Meaning to really take hold.

- We need to bring together groups of stakeholders from every corner of the organization. And report back to the organization throughout the process.

- Selecting our workshop stakeholders is crucially important. This is not a job for the disinterested or the mildly engaged. And there is no room for the perpetually cynical.

- Our stakeholders must be respected by their peers and have the ability to carry a brave, new idea deep into the organization. Choose them wisely. No fewer than five. No more than twelve.

- We need to set expectations with our workshop stakeholders. We do this by helping them understand what is involved, helping them understand what will be required of them, and helping them understand what will be accomplished.

- We have to look at our workshop stakeholders as our audience and promote this to them just as we would promote an idea to our most valuable prospects. We need to help them understand that they have the opportunity to be part of something compelling and profound.

CHAPTER 9
The Big Audacious Meaning clarification process

It's not created. It's revealed.

A Big Audacious Meaning connects to what we're best at, what we're passionate about, and what difference we want to make. In fact, it takes those things and distills them into one powerful, purposeful thought. It can't be manufactured or spun. It has to be something that is genuine to who we are. It may not be readily apparent, but the foundations of our Big Audacious Meaning exist within our organization. It is not something we create. Rather, it is something that is revealed.

Part of this process is depth interviews with the leadership of an organization. During one of these sessions, I had a member of a leadership team say to me, "This organization doesn't have a deeper purpose. The guy who started it just wanted to make money." If you did a cursory investigation of the organization, this assessment would seem to hold true. The founder had not bothered to establish an inspiring ideology and indoctrinate it in the organization. In fact, from his history and all his actions, it was easy to conclude that it was just about the money.

It's never just about the money.

When I had a chance to sit down with the founder of the

organization, some interesting truths began to surface. He believed they could advance the industry in a way that could have a profound impact on the multitude of lives that it touched. He had never given himself permission to let that become a driver for the organization. The foundations of this organization's Big Audacious Meaning had just become a little clearer. It also made me wonder how much further he could have taken the organization if he had given himself the permission to embrace that bigger, more inspiring, world-changing idea.

Past, present, & future

The clarification of our Big Audacious Meaning spans the past, present, and future. Each era offers us unique evidence that will help inform our purpose. Additionally, the discovery within each will help us evaluate the genuineness of the final form of our Big Audacious Meaning.

By looking inward at our organization, we have the opportunity to uncover and rediscover things about ourselves that will help lead us to the difference we hope to make in the world.

This requires digging into our past to understand where we came from. As we dig, it's not unusual to uncover foundational beliefs that helped form the organization at its inception. In other cases, the organization has changed significantly over the course of decades and the founding principles may no longer be as relevant as the day they were introduced. In this situation, we look for the inflection point in the history.

We also want to assess the present state. We want to get a view across the organization (not just in the C-suite). This means talking to people in each of the major divisions. By gathering these viewpoints, we get an understanding of the passions and motivations. And we start to identify differences in perception and understanding. This helps us map the gaps that exist.

We want to look to the future as well. This means engaging those who set the vision for the company. This normally falls to the leadership team. Although, some organizations have stakeholder groups that include employees from across the company that provide guidance. It's good to engage these groups to understand where the organization is headed.

The past: an archeological dig

We're going to go on a dig. A dig to uncover evidence. In this investigation, we're looking for a purpose that may have launched an organization. Sometimes it will be very overt – stated in an original mission. More often than not, we can piece it together from early documents, a study of the decisions made, and more. If the organization is not too old, we've been known to interview retired employees who tell stories of the early days and what drove decisions.

As John Mackey and Rajendra Sisodia explain in their book, *Conscious Capitalism, Liberating the Heroic Spirit of Business*, "Unfortunately, many businesses over time become so preoccupied with surviving, growing, reacting to marketplace changes, or just making money that they forget their purpose. The leadership of such an older business may need to go back and rediscover the company's purpose, much as an archaeologist seeks to discover what brought about a city or a civilization."[40]

For an organization that has been around for decades, it's not unusual that it made a major shift along the way. This is usually after the founders have long passed on the reins. This reset or change of direction is an inflection point worth digging into. When making such a change, organizations very likely document their intent in some way or another.

These are the two places that are most likely to reveal a larger intent – the genesis of the organization and the inflection point.

The archives are the likely place to start. Some organizations keep detailed and organized records of the history. Some have created timelines of the company's past and built elaborate displays or what looks like a small museum. Some even have corporate historians on staff. Others simply have file cabinets full of photos and old documents that nobody has touched for years. In the latter case, hopefully there is somebody around who can identify the people in the pictures and make sense of the significance of the more obscure documents.

We can also survey past news articles and trade magazine mentions as we investigate. The third party stories give us another way to understand what was driving the organization.

It is fascinating to gather all the photos, documents, video, interviews, stories, and more. As we start to look at it as a whole, storylines emerge. Themes take shape. We start to identify the patterns. All of this helps point us to a purpose. Maybe it is something that just got buried along the way. Sometimes it surprises everyone by uncovering a Big Audacious Meaning that was there all along.

It's important to recognize that not all organizations have a long illustrious past. I've done Big Audacious Meaning discoveries with organizations that have been around less than ten years. There is still history there. Don't overlook it. Even digging into this recent past can uncover surprising details.

The only time this archeological investigation does not apply is when working with startups. Obviously, there is no history to dig into. It doesn't mean there isn't lots of purpose-driven thinking that fueled the decision to start something new. But we'll look at that as we next investigate the present.

The present: the state of the union

We are going to look both inside and outside the company as we investigate the present.

We start with the current state of the vision, mission, and values. It is important to start here since these are foundational elements of the organization's ideology. We look at how these ideals are reflected throughout our investigation of the organization.

We also conduct interviews throughout the company. We start with the leadership team to get their views of the purpose behind the organization. While leadership's point of view is important, this is the area of this investigation where we really want to get out and talk to people across all divisions.

Continuing this internal investigation, we examine any internal facing programs the organization conducts, usually through human resources or corporate communications. Additionally, we look at all the good outward-facing efforts that the organization embraces. These include things like the corporate social responsibility program, sustainability efforts, volunteering programs, corporate giving, and more. We want to understand why the organization believes these efforts are important, how they relate to the purpose, and how evident the connections are.

Then we look at how the organization portrays itself. We start with the current brand positioning. We want to understand what drove its formation and the choices made to structure the specific language. We examine all expressions of that brand positioning. We start with the organization's website (or websites) since this has evolved into the nexus of all brand expression and activity. Next, we examine how the brand comes to life through all the outward facing expressions. That manifests itself through all the advertising from traditional media (TV, print, radio, out-of-home, etc.) to one-to-one marketing (email, direct mail, etc.) to search engine marketing, digital media buys, social channel advertising, and more. And we study the PR efforts to understand how we want to align with the demands of today's marketplace forces.

Next, the study turns outward. We want to understand current perceptions and attitudes that influence the organization. We start with any research that the organization has conducted to understand where it stands and any opportunities it has. We also do a survey of recent press about the company to understand any differences between how the organization portrays itself and how the market perceives it. We also want to take a look at the conversations about the organization on the social channels. This view gives us invaluable insight into how individuals relate to the organization, interpret its intent, and more. If the organization has a group of key influencers, we will want to understand their perceptions as well. These can include everything from industry and university experts to community and political leaders.

Finally, we conduct interviews with customers and prospects. This is one of the most important studies we undertake. A Big Audacious Meaning aims to make a difference in a life, a community, or the world. For it to be truly effective, we have to understand what is profoundly important to those we hope to serve.

An enlightening thing happens when we line up what leadership says with what the team members say. With what the organization says and what it does. With what the customers believe and how the rest of the world perceives the organization. Yes, it reveals gaps. But more importantly, it helps us understand the things we will need to do to help our Big Audacious Meaning achieve unquestionable believability.

The future: discovering the intent

To round out our study of the organization, we look to the future. Although we can't predict what will happen, we want to understand the intent of those setting the course. This will help us understand where the organization is headed. This understanding helps us complete the picture. We dug into how the brand evolved from its beginning. We looked at the present state of the affairs. And now we look into the plan for the future.

A good place to start is with any strategic planning that exists. This could be a three to five year plan, the results of a visioning session, and more. Again, we want to understand the intent for the future.

Next, we conduct one-on-one interviews with leadership from across the organization. These sessions allow us to capture the unique point of view of each of these key individuals. We want to understand how each of them perceives the future and how the organization might evolve.

Additionally, we'll examine any insights from consultants and third-party experts that the organization may have engaged in its future planning.

As we aggregate all this insight, we get a clearer picture of where we collectively believe we are headed. From this, we can start to form scenarios about the future.

Analysis & insight

At the end of all this exploration, we find ourselves with a plethora of information. This includes documented plans, company publications, interview transcripts, news stories, anecdotes, and more. Within this information lies the insight that can lead to the Big Audacious Meaning. In some cases, the value of this exploration is to demonstrate the validity of a purpose that has long been present within an organization – just never fully embraced and nurtured.

To bring these insights to light, all this information from our exploration is organized and analyzed. We create a war room of sorts, covering the walls with key pieces of evidence. It could be everything from a picture to a headline to a quote from one of our interviewees. Seeing all the evidence up in one physical space has a unique effect on the ability to see connections emerge. We discover the interrelatedness of seemingly disparate findings. As this happens, primary themes begin to form. And underneath those themes we organize all the evidence.

All of this is compiled in our Exploration Findings Report. More importantly, the insights provide the crucial input for the next phase of our Big Audacious Meaning discovery. The Workshop Sessions.

The pre-workshop preparation

We have already identified and prepped our stakeholders, now we use a pre-workshop survey to gather initial thoughts. This is valuable because it allows each stakeholder to give his her thoughts before introducing the collaborative dynamic of the workshop setting.

There are three questions that help form the structure of our Big Audacious Meaning. Gathering each core stakeholder's answers to these questions provides the input that will fuel our discussion. Here are those questions:

- **"What are we best at?"** This isn't a list of services. It isn't our core competencies. This is verbalizing what we believe is the one thing that we excel at that can make a difference for those we hope to serve.

- **"What are we passionate about?"** What is at the core of what we do? What is it that has the potential to get the whole team excited? Let's put words to that thing that stirs that indescribable feeling in us.

- **"What difference could we make for those we hope to serve?"** This isn't what we do or how we do it. It isn't even the benefit of what we do. This is the benefit of the benefit. This is the profound impact we could have.

Imagine these three questions as a Venn diagram with three circles. In each circle is one of the questions. And in the middle, where those circles overlap, is where we find our Big Audacious Meaning.

The answers are interrelated. In fact, it is how we judge

the validity of each of them. In other words, if we are good at something and passionate about it but it doesn't support how we want to have a profound impact, then we need to rethink our answers. If we are passionate about something and it supports the profound impact we want to have but it isn't what we're good at, then we need to re-evaluate. If we have identified the profound impact we want to have and it is supported by what were good at but it's not something we're passionate about, then we need to adjust our answers until they align.

Our job is to take all this input and prepare it for the workshop session. We'll aggregate and synthesize the answers – combining similar responses and ensuring the language for each answer is clear and compelling. The idea here is to capture the intent or spirit of the answers – not just the exact verbiage our respondents used. Once we do this, we create the workshop boards. At the top of an easel pad sheet, write the question (i.e. What are we best at?). Then list the options that we have synthesized for that question. When we are finished, we should have three easel pad sheets, each with compelling options for each of the Big Audacious Meaning questions.

This prepares us for the next step. The Workshop Session.

The workshop

We begin our workshop by reviewing the key evidence from our exploration of the past, present, and future of the organization, and the resulting conclusions that arose from our insight and analysis. It is inevitable that, through this process, themes have emerged. We share those themes and discuss the potential of each as a group. It's not unusual for the group to be surprised by a theme or two that kept reoccurring through the organization's history or throughout the way it expressed itself. Additionally, we may discover the intersection of themes. Or we may see the opportunity to evolve a theme. All of this good work helps us narrow our examination as a group, leading us toward our Big Audacious Meaning.

Next, we review the results of the pre-workshop survey. We start with the first question – *What are we best at?* We read the options that we have listed on the easel pad sheet. Then we ask the group to vote on the most compelling answer. I like to give each participant a sticker (dot stickers are what I prefer) and ask each to place the sticker next to the answer that they believe best captures the answer to the question for the organization.

We also create a working Big Audacious Meaning statement structure that we fill in as we go. It looks like this:

We _____
(The answer to *What are we best at?*)

So that _____
(The answer to *What are we passionate about?*)

And as a result that _____
(The answer to *What difference could we make?*)

I like to use a whiteboard for this statement because we will find ourselves revising and refining the statement as we go. It's also good to note that we don't expect to develop the final language for the Big Audacious Meaning statement in this workshop. It is impossible to craft the most powerful language in a group setting.

Our job is to capture the spirit of what we want our statement to say. We'll refine later. That's why I call this a *working* Big Audacious Meaning statement

We complete this review-vote-document process for each of the three questions. When we get to the third question, I like to add in an exercise called the 5 Whys. I've found that stakeholders tend to hold back a bit on their answer to the question, *"What difference could we make for those we hope to serve?"* It's understandable. After all, it's not every day that we are asked to identify something so inherently profound. The 5 Whys helps coax out the most deeply meaningful answer.

Officially, the 5 Whys technique was developed by Taiichi Ohno, the father of the Toyota Production System. Ohno developed the technique as a systematic problem-solving tool. It helped go beyond the symptoms to getting to the root cause of the problem. So, when you addressed the problem, you weren't just putting a Band-Aid on it. You were developing a solution that would really solve it. In our search for purpose, we're not using the technique to get to the root of problem. Instead, we're using it to uncover the most profound difference we will make in a life, a community, or even the world. Asking 'why' helps us get past the short-term and functional goals. We can start by asking, "Why do we exist?" It's not unusual to get an answer like, "To maximize our shareholders' value." Or, "To help our customers solve their problems." Neither of these is the ultimate answer we're looking for. But they are valid as a start. Now we just need to keep asking "why" to get to that Big Audacious Meaning.

Here is an example from Kansas City Young Audiences. The organization promotes the developmental power that the arts provide in children's lives. Here is how our 5 Why's exploration went:

- **Why does Kansas City Young Audiences exist?**
  To creatively engage kids in learning through the arts.

- **Why?**
  So they can build critical thinking, communication, & collaboration skills.

- **Why?**
  So they can discover new ways to think and learn.

- **Why?**
  So they can experience the spark - that transformative "a-ha" moment when they grasp an idea or discover a new talent.

- **Why?**
  So they can carry that spark out into the world and transform lives that they touch.

We could have stopped anywhere along the way in this process and called that our purpose. But it would not have been as profound. It would not have been a Big Audacious Meaning.

The Big Audacious Meaning

The 5 Whys is almost magical in its ability to help us zero in on that profound thought that will become our Big Audacious Meaning. It's good to note again that the language may not be in its final form. The essence of the thought won't change. But we will hone the language to make sure it is in its most clear and powerful form.

With Kansas City Young Audiences, the 5th why brought us to the answer, "So they can carry that spark out into the world and transform lives that they touch."

In the end, that was turned into a Big Audacious Meaning that answered the three questions:

- What are we best at? (Helping kids experience that spark.)

- What are we passionate about? (Transforming lives through the arts.)

- What difference could we make in a life, a community, or even the world? (Helping those kids carry that spark out into the world and transform lives.)

Ultimately, the Big Audacious Meaning for Kansas City Young Audiences was crafted as this:

"To help kids experience the transformative power of the arts so they can carry that spark out into the world and transform lives that they touch."

Here is another example that came out of my work with First Federal Bank.

- What are we best at? (Helping people achieve financial wellbeing.)

- What are we passionate about? (Helping improve lives and communities.)

- What difference could we make in a life, a community, or even the world? (Creating an environment where we can all prosper together.)

For First Federal, we refined the statement of the Big Audacious Meaning to this:

To help people achieve financial wellbeing in order to improve lives and communities – so that we can all prosper together.

The Big Audacious Meaning is unparalleled in its ability to capture this exceptional expression. This game-changing belief that is the core of the organization's story.

The Four Forces

After clarifying our Big Audacious Meaning, we have an opportunity to solidify its importance with this influential group of stakeholders that we have gathered. In order to do that, we run an exercise called The Four Forces.

This exercise helps the group build a sense of ownership in the purpose that we have just clarified. That's important because when they begin to have ownership, we speed adoption.

Each of The Four Forces poses a question about our Big Audacious Meaning. Our aim is to define why our purpose is exceptional when viewed through the lens of each.

- Force One: The Individual – Why is our purpose valuable to the individuals we hope to serve?

- Force Two: Our Organization – Why is our purpose believable coming from our organization?

- Force Three: Our Peers – Why is our purpose unique among our peers?

- Force Four: The World – Why is our purpose relevant in today's world?

By having our stakeholders answer these questions, we begin the process of them buying in. And give them the tools to help others in the organization buy into our Big Audacious Meaning.

To conduct the exercise, we put each question at the top of an easel pad sheet. Starting with the first question, we ask the group, "Why is our purpose valuable to the individuals we hope to serve? As our group generates answers, we write them on Post-it Notes and put those notes up on the easel pad sheet. I like using the Post-it Notes because we may discover as we go that we want to move an answer because it fits better under one of the other Four Forces questions.

Once we have gone through all four of the Four Forces questions, we give each member of the group a sticker for each of the questions and ask them to select the most compelling answer for each by placing their stickers next to their choices.

For each of the questions, we review the biggest vote getters with the group. This leads to that buy-in we talked about by illustrating to them how they have helped identify the profound impact of our Big Audacious Meaning – with the individuals we hope to serve, in our organization, among our peer group, and in today's world.

In addition to this, we can use the insight they have helped create as we introduce our Big Audacious Meaning to our organization and then to the world.

Piloting purpose in an organization

Not every organization is ready to go through the purpose clarification process. I have had excited Chief Marketing Officers or leaders of business units that wanted to explore what defining a

Big Audacious Meaning could do for them. But they didn't have the top leadership on board. Are they just out of luck until they can win over a CEO?

Not necessarily.

A profound purpose can transform a brand. And not just the organizational brand. It can be applied at the divisional level. Even on down to the product level. Just because the organization hasn't adopted a purpose doesn't mean a Big Audacious Meaning can't be piloted at these lower levels. Think of it as an opportunity to prototype the purpose.

The effect it will have on those brands at the lower levels will be powerful. Our brand will go beyond trying to win prospects on our attributes (what we do or how we do it). Our brand will even go beyond focusing on the benefits of those attributes. It will embrace the benefit of the benefit. That profound difference our brand can have on a life, a community, or even the world.

That is an idea that is potent enough to rise up in an organization and become the foundational principle that inspires everything the company does.

Many times, organizations have good alignment between the guiding principles at the very top of the organization (driving strategy and culture) and the principles driving things at the divisional level or even the product level. The organization may not have gone through the process of formally clarifying its Big Audacious Meaning. But, there is a tacit alignment. It is in these situations where prototyping a purpose at the divisional or product level could lead to a Big Audacious Meaning that eventually could spread across the entire organization. But remember. This is possible because that tacit alignment exists.

Say the organization does not have the tacit alignment that I talked about. Is it worth pursuing a Big Audacious Meaning at the divisional or product level? Absolutely.

We will build a more powerful story framework for the offerings. Furthermore, we will build impassioned believers among our team who help us push things to new heights. And they will attract like-minded believers, helping us recruit the best and the brightest to our efforts.

That's a pretty awesome worst-case scenario for pursuing a Big Audacious Meaning.

A word of caution

Once we have identified our Big Audacious Meaning, something inevitably happens. The rational side of us wants to get in on the action. It's not unusual to want to start citing facts and figures to help prove the validity of our belief. In some cases, doubt creeps in and we worry that our Big Audacious Meaning may threaten our ability to be taken seriously.

So we build a case.

It's important to give our belief an acid test. It's important to gather the quantitative proof. It helps us confidently and boldly push forward, knowing we have unassailable proof to dispel the criticisms of anyone who would take shots at us. But, too often, we let this overwhelm the magic we all felt when we clarified the Big Audacious Meaning.

We find our storytelling gets reduced to statistics and rational arguments. We may even believe that our facts and figures are so compelling that they give us a free pass from having to navigate the messy human stuff. We tell ourselves that the numbers speak for themselves. And that they're quantifiable. No need to negotiate the decidedly squishier terrain of stories and emotions.

Thus, the erosion starts. Our Big Audacious Meaning begins to feel not all that inspiring. And we can't seem to get anyone else excited about it. It doesn't feel so undeniable anymore.

This is why the first thing we should do is create our anthem.

Creating our anthem

With our Big Audacious Meaning identified, it's now time to give it a voice. We have just been through an amazing journey. We have clarified something that will proclaim how we will have a profound impact on the lives of those around us. We need to capture this monumental idea in a form that honors the magnitude. Builds belief. Sparks imagination. And inspires all to join us on this quest.

This is not a memo we send out to the staff to announce that we've established a purpose. It's not even a mission statement (I think we've covered the problem with those.) This task demands a unique form. One that can capture the depth and magnitude. One that we can fill with meaning.

We need an anthem.

An anthem speaks to the big challenge that lies ahead. It proclaims the difference we will make. And paints a picture of the profound impact that we will have.

It's one page. And devoid of jargon and corporate speak. Rather it is the bold manifesto that turns people into believers. Believers into advocates. And advocates into evangelists.

This is the most powerful expression of our Big Audacious Meaning. It will become our touchstone from this day forward.

It will help us all make decisions up and down the organization. Everyday.

It should be that fundamental. And so inspiring that we all want to keep it near so it can guide us or jolt us out of our complacency.

Shooting the movie

The language of our anthem is potent. Now imagine combining it with equally moving images and music that sweeps us up and allows us to lose ourselves in this big audacious idea.

Something special happens when you create this two-minute cinematic wonder. It can speed adoption, helping everyone understand the difference the organization will make in a life, a community, or even the world. Most importantly, it can induce those goose bumps that the core stakeholder team first felt when the idea emerged. That can help the passion go viral through an organization.

There are many ways to do this. You can demonstrate the idea with inspiring images – tell a wonderful story and watch what happens. Another way is to go out and interview team members around the company. Introduce the new Big Audacious Meaning to them. Then ask them what this could mean to them. Talk to them about their hopes and aspirations. Making that part of your purpose movie can make it nothing short of riveting.

I've seen people moved to tears as a Big Audacious Meaning comes to life on the screen. Maybe it's because it connects with people's desire to do something with real meaning. To make a difference. Or maybe because it gives people such an incredible sense of hope and excitement for the future.

It will be there to inspire recruits, too. Want to woo talented team members? Show them the movie about the purpose that they can be part of. Let them get swept up in the difference they can help make in the world.

Many times, this anthem movie finds a home on the organization's website. It can communicate so much to everyone from prospects to investors. The anthem movie has unrivaled powers.

Crafting the rallying cry

There is one more element to consider as we are giving our Big Audacious Meaning a voice. It is the rallying cry.

The rallying cry is the shorthand for our Big Audacious Meaning. It distills this powerful idea down to its most succinct form. Imagine three to seven words that capture that magic. That's a tall order. But when done well, it can become one of the most recognizable expressions of our purpose. It can even feel like a call to arms to join the movement. We don't have to look any further than Nike's "Just do it." to recognize the power of a rallying cry.

As you would imagine, this is no mere tagline. A tagline sounds like an afterthought. Like it is something you tack on to your brand.

On the other hand, a rallying cry sounds bold and energizing. A rallying cry invites us into the story. It taps into our aspirations. It charges us to become better. It does all this and more. Just look at Apple. They told us to "Think different." As a rallying cry, this encapsulated Apple's purpose of helping people unlock their creativity and innovation. This kind of rallying cry inspires us to imagine ourselves in a different state. In this case, one where we do amazing things. Engaging people in this way is incredibly compelling. That's why leading organizations take the time to hone this invaluable asset.

Getting the words right

The words we use to bring our Big Audacious Meaning to life are crucial. The good news is that we all write. The bad news is that we all write.

Early in our life, we are all taught to write. Anybody who can pick up a pencil can participate. It's not like drawing. Here, we make a greater distinction between who can draw and who can't. But putting words to paper feels more democratic. Everyone can write.

This is a wonderful thing. Because it encourages us all to add our ideas. This is a troublesome thing as well. Because very few are great at reducing a powerful sentiment to just a few goose bumps-inducing words.

Words are powerful. Walt Disney said, "If you dream it, you can do it." Harry Truman had a sign on his desk that read, "The buck stops here." And John F. Kennedy asked us, "If not us, who? If not now, when?"

It doesn't take pages upon pages of words to inspire. In fact, those who reduce a sentiment down to just a few words are the ones we quote. They are the ones that inspire us.

Finding the right words requires more than a good thesaurus. It also requires the use of a good deal of restraint. It's as much what we leave out as what we add in.

This is where the challenge becomes evident. We all have ideas we feel compelled to add. But few of us are great editors.

It is the editing we need. To weed out the distracting language.

To get to the heart of the idea. To communicate with deep meaning. And to inspire interpretation. This makes our words engaging, meaningful, and sustainable.

Chip and Dan Heath give a great explanation of the power of this ability, "Coming up with a short compact phrase is easy. Anybody can do it. On the other hand, coming up with a profound compact phrase is incredibly difficult."[41]

Is this a tall order? To create something engaging, meaningful, and sustainable with just a handful of words?

Yes.

Is it worth the trouble? We have to ask ourselves what we want those words to do. If we're creating a mission statement so we can check off the mission statement box, then let's not bother. But if we are looking for more than a mission. If we're looking for people to believe in what we're doing. If we're looking to create a movement. Then we need to choose our words very, very carefully.

Who knows, someday somebody may be quoting us.

Key Takeaways

- A Big Audacious Meaning exists within our organization. It is not something we create. Rather, it is something that is revealed by digging into our past, assessing our present state, and looking to the future.

- All the findings and insights of our discovery will be used in the Workshop Session. They are also compiled in our Exploration Findings Report.

- To prepare for the workshop, we conduct a survey to gather input to the three questions that define a Big Audacious Meaning – What are we best at? What are we passionate about? And what difference could we make for those we hope to serve?

- During the workshop we will review and discuss the key evidence from our discovery. We will also review and discuss the input from a pre-workshop survey. All of this helps us refine the statement of our Big Audacious Meaning.

- We use the 5 Whys technique to help uncover the most profound difference we will make in a life, a community, or even the world.

- After clarifying our Big Audacious Meaning, we run The Four Forces exercise to help the group build a sense of ownership in the newly clarified purpose.

- With our Big Audacious Meaning in place, we create our anthem, our anthem movie, and a rallying cry.

SECTION 5: TRANSFORMING EVERYTHING

Chapter 10
Bringing purpose into our brand

Clarifying our Big Audacious Meaning is highly emotional. Something that is well suited to human beings, but not so much corporations.

Corporations aren't human. For good reason. They need to provide structure, because we humans can be messy and unpredictable.

The order and structure that corporations provide allow everyone to operate as a team rather than tripping over each other. Their value is in their lack of humanness. Which is great if you're thinking about logistics. But not so great if you're thinking about purpose.

On the other hand, we often talk about brands as living and breathing things. When we develop a brand, we define a personality and a voice. We make it as human as possible. Because us humans have a higher likelihood to relate to things that feel human. Additionally, viable brands adapt and evolve with the world around them. Much like humans. Yes, corporations evolve as well. But not with the fluidity that brands display.

In essence, brands are more human than corporations. So when we think about how something as humanly inspiring as purpose should be expressed, it only makes sense that it should be with the brand rather than in corporate governance documents.

That said, not all brands are ready for a Big Audacious

Meaning. It requires an evolution. Some get there in a relatively short period of time. Think of Toms – which is shorthand for 'tomorrow's shoes' – a brand conceived with the idea that it could sell you a pair of shoes today and give away a pair to someone in need tomorrow.

Then there are brands that get there over time. Dove wasn't necessarily a name that evoked a Big Audacious Meaning when it first emerged. But today it represents something bigger and deeper.

Both of these are examples of brands that have embraced a Big Audacious Meaning. These are highly evolved brands that arrived at this point taking two different roads.

Brands generally find themselves in one of four levels. From the neophyte where very little meaning exists to the advanced where a Big Audacious Meaning can give a brand magical powers.

Level 1 brand - Who you are

Defining who you are is the beginner level of the branding world. Its primary concern is giving the organization an identity (a name and maybe a mark) that hasn't been claimed by another company in the vicinity. It does little to differentiate – we recognize that Bob's Plumbing is different from Joe's Plumbing, but we don't know why it's different beyond the name.

With no focus on real and meaningful differentiation, Stage 1 brands resort to crazy stunts to get attention. This probably explains the entire giant inflatables industry. You know, things like the giant blow up gorilla that used car lots and such place on their building to lure passersby onto the property. There's no real benefit to the unsuspecting sucker who wanders onto the lot. It just makes them curious as to why there is a two story primate waving to them from the roof of that building.

This also reminds me of another weird byproduct that affected Stage 1 brands in days gone by. There was a time when the Yellow Pages ruled the way businesses got found. This had such an influence on businesses that they actually chose their name so they would be listed first in the Yellow Pages. That's how we got a whole lot of companies named AAA (insert type of company). In other words, AAA Plumbing or AAA Catering. By putting 'AAA' in the name it virtually guaranteed that you would get the first listing in the Yellow Pages, beating out Quality Plumbing or Delicious Dining Catering.

While this may offer some benefit when it comes to alphabetical listings, it actually hamstrings the brand in the long run. The generic AAA-insert-business-type name does nothing to impart any distinctiveness. It's just a generic name. It forfeits a long-term opportunity to create uniqueness for a limited tactical gain.

This is typical of Stage 1 branding. It is utilitarian. It doesn't help us understand what makes the organization different or if there is a benefit to be derived. Quite simply, the brand really doesn't have much meaning. As such, it doesn't tell us much more than the company exists.

Level 2 brand - What you do

Level 2 branding begins to recognize that establishing differentiation can help separate an offering in the minds of prospects. It is an approach that relies on describing what you do or how you do it. This results in a list of attributes that can support the claim of what makes the brand unique.

While this sounds quite rational in theory, it is proving problematic in practice. With competition today, it is difficult to have a truly clear set of unique attributes. Even if a brand accomplishes this, it is difficult to sustain because of the speed of innovation. Other organizations can quickly spin up capabilities, neutralizing what was once a competitor's unique set of attributes.

A large number of organizations operate at level 2. It helps create a foundation for fundamental marketing efforts without requiring much branding sophistication. It's like my auto mechanic who has a sign that says they do oil changes, brake jobs, etc. It's good they let everyone know what they do. But there is not much there that tells us why we should choose them as opposed to those grease monkeys across the street. Many small businesses never evolve beyond this level because of the associated demands that they can't or won't meet (either financially, strategically, or both.)

As a result, we may have a vague idea of what they do. But most of the time, we are forced to figure out why that is different than another option. And we very rarely do. This leads us to view these businesses as much the same, and treat them like a commodity – making our decision to engage with them one based largely on price alone. That makes it more difficult for these businesses to create the margins they desire as they tussle with competitors in the downward spiral of pricing battles.

Level 3 brand - What you do for your prospects

Advanced brands begin at level 3. These are brands that understand the strategic advantage of differentiating on the benefit they provide to their prospects. They go beyond what they do or how they do it to help people understand what effect those things will have on their lives. These benefits can be expressed rationally - "We save you time". But the more powerful benefits have an emotional pull - "We free up time giving you more of those precious moments to share with those that you love".

It's easy to stay detached when presented with a purely rational decision. An emotional appeal reaches beyond that easy detachment, connecting with that part of us where aspirations reside. When a brand connects with this part of us, it feels more relevant, more meaningful, and more valuable.

Advanced brands understand the power of putting themselves in the shoes of those they serve. Of understanding what's really important in these people's lives. And then offering something that speaks to the heart as well as the head.

Neophytes view the brand as a necessary evil in the process of selling something to someone ("We have to have a name and then tell people what we do.") Advanced brands focus on how we might help someone. They ask, "What can we do to help you achieve your dreams?" By doing this we develop a relationship with a person that is much more meaningful than a transaction.

There are amazing benefits of creating a brand that nurtures this relationship. It can blunt the sensationalism of a new entrant into the market. It can help fend off the effects of a competitor slashing prices. It can do all these things because it develops trust.

Advanced brands understand the importance of this. Trust is something you can't buy or manufacture. It has to be built and earned by having a relentless focus on the desires of those you serve. But once you have it, you can accelerate everything.

Level 4 brand - The difference you make

The highest level of branding asks, "What difference will we make in a life, a community, or even the world?" This is our Big Audacious Meaning.

This orientation is light years away from the neophyte's "necessary evil" view of branding. And it is the full evolution of the advanced brand.

Here, the brand is steeped in a profound purpose. That means all positioning of the brand is founded in purpose as well. That's important to note for a couple of reasons. First, a brand's position will need to adapt as competitive pressure and other market forces change. A brand founded in purpose can move quickly and confidently to an advantageous position. There is no anxiety that comes with feeling like we have to rethink the brand. We have our core established. The repositioning is just a strategic maneuver guided by our Big Audacious Meaning. Second, our positioning gets stronger. With our Big Audacious Meaning at our core, we free ourselves from quibbling with competitors over whose functional differentiation is superior. Because we have something much more meaningful and relevant behind our position. We have purpose.

Most of all, we create a brand that does more than just differentiate. It inspires. It inspires team members as well as prospects and customers. Unlike all the other levels of branding, it is the one that has the greatest potential for turning those team members, prospects, and customers into advocates and even evangelists.

Your Big Audacious Meaning doesn't have to save the world

Embracing a Big Audacious Meaning can seem daunting. It's awesome to have the ambition to make a big difference in the world. But it doesn't have to start that way. Sometimes a smaller meaningful and worthwhile idea can grow into a movement. Look at Starbucks for example. The Starbucks brand isn't just about a good cup of coffee. The brand became all about a cool little oasis where people can treat themselves to a small getaway. It was expressed in the coffee as well as the environment (design, music, people, and more). Officially, Starbucks states it in their *mission*: "To inspire and nurture the human spirit – one person, one cup and one neighborhood at a time."[42]

That's not necessarily a world-changing idea. But it resonated with a population that maybe felt overworked and underappreciated. People have become passionate about the brand because it gives them something they had been longing for. That's pretty awesome to help people feel a little better in the course of their day. And that, perhaps, is really the larger meaning that Starbucks doesn't state. For this mission to become a Big Audacious Meaning, we just need to ask, "Why?" Why is it important to inspire and nurture the human spirit? I'd contend that it lifts us up, making it more likely that we will lift up those around us. Or maybe it's as simple as saying that it makes us all a little kinder to each other. Imagine making that part of what you do. Spreading a little more kindness in the world.

What if Starbucks became an advocate for that? What if that became their Big Audacious Meaning? Imagine walking into a Starbucks feeling like you weren't only treating yourself, but you were also part of a movement to lift up others or to spread more kindness in the world.

Here is another example of how a Big Audacious Meaning can begin at a very personal level. My firm was working with an insurance company that knew it had a bigger purpose than just creating another insurance offering. This new brand could have said that it existed to help customers protect against the unexpected. That's what you'd anticipate from a me-too insurance company. And you'd probably yawn and move on if you heard that.

We worked together to clarify a Big Audacious Meaning. We helped them discover that their purpose wasn't just to help people play defense. The purpose was to help people advance. To make the most of life. Think about that. What could a person do knowing they had an advocate who was helping them advance rather than just protect. The brand set out to help people imagine what life could be. And then helped them work toward it. That meant developing ways to stay connected to that person after they bought a policy. And offering useful tools and information that weren't just about insurance, but included things that helped them build a better life. That's a purpose full of meaning. Meaning that can make a big difference in a person's life.

Imagine coming to work every day for this organization, believing you are not just selling insurance, but that you are helping a fellow human being make the most of life – for her and her family.

Your Big Audacious Meaning makes this possible. Whether you're setting out to change the world or just make one life a little better.

Before we buy, we want to know why

People don't buy our products and services. They buy what those products can help them become. This is the fundamental truth that makes a Big Audacious Meaning undeniably important. There is a great summary on a post at useronboard.com that captures this thought quite elegantly: "People don't buy products; they buy better versions of themselves."[43]

We all have our favorite brand or brands. They are the ones that have the ability to connect with us. Many times it's in a way that's indescribable. We just know that it feels right.

What is it that they do that builds that connection? They understand their meaning and where it comes from. And knowing that is what powers an extraordinary story and an extraordinary connection.

When a brand has a clearly stated and engaging purpose, it gives us a reason to connect. Studies even show that people will go out of their way to choose a brand that has a purpose that they can appreciate and even get behind.

As Joey Reiman writes, "We no longer buy it, but rather we buy into it, because it stands for something greater."[44]

Of course, it has to be authentic. You can't just manufacture a "why" and expect people to rush to your door. In today's transparent world, it's too easy to see through the hollow words. Your "why" has to be demonstrated. Through what you do, what you share, and how you help.

The great news is that once you unearth your "why", your stories become more powerful. More meaningful. And you have the opportunity to do something that every brand strives for. To not only convert prospects, but to turn them into evangelists.

Purpose unlocks the benefit of the benefit

Clarifying a profound purpose has a powerful effect on our ability to win the hearts and minds of prospects. Because when we incorporate this purpose into our message, we unlock the ability to go beyond features. To even go beyond benefits. We develop that rare ability to champion the benefit of the benefit.

Let's say we are manufacturers of light bulbs and we want to find the most compelling way to convert prospects into customers. We could tell people about what we do. We could talk about the watts. We could talk about color temperature or our quality manufacturing process. This is where the majority of organizations play, quibbling over whose features or processes are superior. Does this have an effect on our customers? Absolutely. It makes their eyes glaze over.

The next step up would be to talk about what those features deliver. Which, when you think about it, is what potential customers are really after. Our customers don't want to buy a light bulb. What they really want is what that light from the bulb helps them do. That light helps Mr. Prospect find the TV remote (rather than fumbling around in the dark.) It also gives a warm glow to his home, making it seem inviting and friendly. Rather than light bulb mechanics, we would talk about the benefit – what that light does for the quality of life. Emphasizing the benefit begins to give our prospects a reason to care.

But what if we took it further? What if we took it to a place where things get magical? That's what happens when we bring purpose into the equation. Imagine that before developing our story, our organization goes through the purpose clarification process. Out of that process, we uncover the deeper purpose of our light bulb company - that profound difference we can make. We would express it like this:

"We illuminate lives, helping people discover the everyday wonders around them. It may be in the words of that novel that you've curled up with. Or maybe it's in the pinkness of your baby daughter's cheeks and the way her face lights up as you cradle her in your lap. These are the moments that make our lives. And we are here to make sure you don't miss a moment."

In this example, it's no longer just about our watts and manufacturing processes. It's no longer just about the light our bulbs create. It's about something bigger. The purpose is about being an advocate. It's about shining a light on those moments that make life rich and full of wonder.

That is the benefit of the benefit.

Imagine what happens when that enters our story. Imagine the reaction we create when we speak to the profound difference we can have by helping people focus on illuminating those moments in their lives. Could it help spread a little joy in our world? Could it help us become a catalyst for celebrating those things that help us shine as humans?

Imagine the messages that would flow from this purpose-driven position. But don't stop at the messaging. Imagine sponsoring a program that encourages kids to read every night (when our light bulbs do their thing). Imagine what that would do for our team members. It would help transform them from makers of light bulbs to the ones who illuminate those special moments in people's lives. Imagine what kind of recruits we could attract.

We can only go so far if we just stick to the features. We can go further by finding the benefits. But if we really want things to open up, we need to get to our profound purpose. And then let it lead us to the benefit of the benefit.

Key Takeaways

- When we think about how something as humanly inspiring as purpose should be expressed, it only makes sense that it should be with the brand rather than in corporate governance documents.

- Brands generally find themselves in one of four levels. At Level 1, the brand forms an identity, but does little to differentiate itself. At Level 2, the brand focuses on what it does or how it does it, but still leaves us to figure out why it's different. At Level 3, the brand focuses on what it does for the prospect, highlighting the benefit of the brand to create differentiation. At Level 4, the brand incorporates a Big Audacious Meaning to create an irresistible uniqueness.

- Your Big Audacious Meaning doesn't have to save the world. It can start small, making a difference one life at a time.

- People don't buy our products and services. They buy what those products can help them become.

- When we incorporate purpose into our message, we unlock the ability to go beyond features. To even go beyond benefits. We develop that rare ability to champion the benefit of the benefit.

CHAPTER 11
Creating believers

Clarifying our Big Audacious Meaning is the culmination of an exceptional journey. So there should be an appropriate amount of basking in the glow of our accomplishment. But after all the backslapping and other well deserved self-congratulatory acts, we need to actually do something with that purpose.

John Mackey and Rajendra Sisodia elaborate, "To succeed, the business must work on the implementation of purpose on an ongoing basis. The work must involve all levels of the organization, so that the entire company feels invested and energized. The purpose must be integrated into orientation processes and new team member training programs. It also needs to be explained to customers and to the media. Leaders must take purpose into account in making all important decisions. For example, purpose should be integrated into performance evaluations, R&D, and strategic planning."[45]

Everything should be built on an undeniable and irresistible sense of purpose. It should be at the heart of everything an organization does. Which means it should be declared. Boldly. First, across the organization. Then with customers, partners, and investors. And then, to the world. But we're just beginning. Because it's not just what we say, it's what we do.

Purpose must be proven. It must be lived.

At the very heart of purpose is the desire to make a difference in a life. In other words, to serve. So after we define the purpose, we must develop the things that prove our purpose is real. Things that demonstrate our desire to serve. For example, that could include a program that generously educates customers and prospects.

It could influence how products are made or evolved. It could mean changing the way team members engage customers. And more. All these things have one thing in common. They demonstrate that this is more than spin. More than a gimmick. They demonstrate how we live our purpose.

Before he hired me to help him clarify his organization's purpose, I had a CEO ask me a very simple question, "What do we do after we clarify it?" Now I have some very elaborate models of how a Big Audacious Meaning becomes inculcated throughout an organization's ecosystem and then propagated out into the larger world. I could have given him the 45-minute slide presentation, complete with me stalking about and waving my arms quite vigorously from time to time. But he had already had some introduction to what I do, and I don't think he was just randomly looking for an excuse to sit through 45 minutes of my shenanigans. He was looking for the bridge between clarifying a Big Audacious Meaning and it becoming real.

"We have to ensure our people are true believers first." was my response.

If we as an organization do not genuinely embrace it, then how can we expect anyone else to do the same? It was also the answer he needed to hear out loud. We all need to become believers. And so, that is where we will begin.

Making it a big deal

So we have our Big Audacious Meaning and we're ready to unveil its final form to the organization. This should be that big moment where we pull back the curtain and hear the audible gasps of the audience as they experience our Big Audacious Meaning for the first time. You may think that expecting audible gasps is a bit much, but I've been there when the anthem was read or the movie was shared. I've seen longtime employees giddy with excitement. The message here is do not underestimate the power of this moment. People have been waiting a long time for a reason to believe like this - sometimes the length of entire careers. Embrace and celebrate the moment.

I had one client that invited the entire team to a major league soccer stadium to reveal their Big Audacious Meaning. This coincided with a complete brand makeover as well. After playing their movie, the stadium scoreboards lit up with their new logo that reflected the Big Audacious Meaning. There was an audible gasp.

How could you not feel a sense of pride in your organization when they announce something so momentous and do it in such a spectacular way? Standing in the glow of those scoreboards, you could not help but feel that great things lie ahead.

In another instance, I had a client who took the show on the road. With geographically distributed locations, it was difficult to get everyone in the same venue. So they took the show to them. This had some equally powerful effects as the big stadium reveal. First, it demonstrated that the organization believed these people were important. And second, it gave incredible weight to the message. After all, the head guy had come to them.

Both of these examples used an impactful physical demonstration. One capitalized on an awe-inspiring venue. The other took advantage of an unexpected act of a leader. In both, the organizations recognized that they needed an act that honored the magnitude of a Big Audacious Meaning.

Owning the anthem

At the center of both these examples is the anthem. Whether it is read as an anthem or brought to life in the movie. Or both.

The anthem is the core expression of the Big Audacious Meaning. Unfortunately, after a successful launch event, it's too easy to let the anthem slide into oblivion. Something that important should be kept front and center.

I like to recommend that the anthem be put into a form that everyone wants to keep at hand. Most often, that becomes a well-designed piece that gets pinned up in offices and cubicles. We have also created a pocket-sized handbook that tells the story of the Big Audacious Meaning, including the anthem.

No matter what form it takes, it needs to be well designed. Excellent design ensures that it will get displayed, and it telegraphs the importance of the anthem.

Our #1 prospect

Good marketers know that they need to expose people to an idea multiple times before they can expect that idea to start to take hold. I've seen good organizations that practice this, but totally forget the principle when it comes to winning the hearts and minds of their own people.

We can't take our own people for granted. A Big Audacious Meaning is monumentally important. But if we give it the one-and-done treatment, it will become the "initiative du jour" in our team's minds. After the glow of the big reveal fades, we start to hear things like, "Yeah, this is another one of those management things. Next month it will be something else."

Lisa Earle McLeod expands on this idea, "People want to be part of something bigger than themselves. But how many of us have been burned in the past? We're all familiar with flavor-of-the-month initiatives. And let's be honest, at some point in our careers, many of us have worked for self-serving jerks who loved to give lip service to the newest management fads and trends."[46]

This would be a terrible fate for our Big Audacious Meaning. Imagine trying to recapture our people's enthusiasm after that.

We need a concerted effort directed first and foremost to our people. We need to plan and budget for it. And execute it with the same dogged determination that drives our efforts with building believers outside the organization. I recommend a yearlong introductory effort. This length of time allows us to create a quantity of exposures to build retention among our team. More importantly, it gives us a way to demonstrate that this is a big deal that the organization is committed to. That should be followed with a yearly sustaining plan that ensures our Big Audacious Meaning stays in the hearts and minds of our most important constituents.

In fact, take this task out of the hands of HR or even Corporate Communications and have the creative minds in Marketing handle this. Portray it as a campaign to win the hearts and minds of our most critical audience.

There are two things we must do. First, we must make our Big Audacious Meaning relevant. That means telling stories. And giving concrete examples to illustrate how this purpose comes to life in the everyday. As the months pass, we will be able to gather real stories from our team members that highlight how it is taking hold and how real people in the organization are embodying the purpose.

A post on the Harvard Business Review site explains the importance of this, "We know that people are substantially more motivated by their organization's transcendent purpose (how it improves lives) than by its transactional purpose (how it sells goods and services). Transcendent purpose is effectively communicated through stories – for example, by describing the pitiable situations of actual, named customers and how their problems were solved by your efforts."[47]

Second, we must maintain the enthusiasm. Our Big Audacious Meaning can't be relegated to a mention in the third bullet of a monthly employee email. It needs to stand apart. And we need to incorporate surprise and delight. That means doing the unexpected from time to time. One organization that I worked with would hold impromptu events that rallied the troops around the Big Audacious Meaning. It's these unexpected and delight-full actions that can reenergize everyone when it may feel like enthusiasm is waning.

In addition to all this, I always recommend creating a Big Audacious Meaning team member advisory board. Have them meet quarterly to:

- Suggest ways that we can amplify our purpose

- Identify pain points or roadblocks that are keeping our purpose from flourishing

- Share ideas from others across the organization

These key team members can become invaluable ambassadors for our Big Audacious Meaning. We need to choose them carefully. And we need to engage them with excitement and energy, stoking their fire for our purpose. Most of all, we need to make sure they are seeing their input result in real progress, otherwise we risk losing the passion of these key influencers.

There is an irresistible pull to the idea that there is a difference that we can make. And there is untold potential in the pursuit of that purpose. Tapping that potential starts within the organization. That's what makes this internal effort so vital. It can accelerate the speed at which a Big Audacious Meaning is fully embraced, amplifying understanding of the purpose and its power. If we want to shorten the timeline to creating evangelists within the organization, this is the ticket.

Creating a movement

We are all susceptible to the need to belong. We are comforted by belonging. We seek it, whether we realize it or not. It is a fundamental human desire. Research shows that it affects everything from our health to our happiness.

This should not be surprising to any of us. We can all identify instances in our own lives where we have sought out belonging.

In his book, *Start with Why: How Great Leaders Inspire Everyone to Take Action*, Simon Sinek gives an insightful explanation, "When companies talk about WHAT they do and how advanced their products are, they may have appeal, but they do not necessarily represent something to which we want to belong. But when a company clearly communicates its WHY, what they believe, and we believe what they believe, then we will sometimes go to extraordinary lengths to include those products or brands in our lives."[48]

A Big Audacious Meaning creates a connectedness where our

believers feel like they are pursuing something with us that can make a real difference in the world.

Harley Davidson was on the brink of bankruptcy twice in the latter half of last century. There were a number of reasons. An attempt to scale production at the expense of quality. The intrusion of foreigner competitors into the market. And more.

Harley Davidson was able to survive situations that would have crushed others because of a sense of belonging among the brand's believers. To them, it wasn't just a brand of motorcycle, it was a symbol of rugged individualism. A symbol of freedom. A symbol of America.

The revitalization of the brand in the 1980's leaned heavily on this powerful sense of belonging. Harley Davidson created the Harley Owners Group (HOG) to help owners not only connect with the brand, but also with each other. It used that connectedness to create rides to raise funds for charity (the brand has addressed challenges including muscular dystrophy and hunger).

The brand championed this belonging. It was a purpose that fulfilled a need for an entire community of believers. In fact, 'believers' may not do this group justice. It may be more appropriate to refer to them as 'fanatics'. After all, Harley Davidson is one of the rare brands that you will find tattooed on the arms of its believers. People will literally 'brand' themselves as part of the Harley Davidson clan.

Ignore belonging at your own peril

I watched a powerful board member of a Fortune 500 company orchestrate the ouster of the company's CEO who had a long-range vision for creating the connectedness I've been talking about. He then had the CEO replaced with someone who would execute his plan for optimizing quarterly returns. Rather than embrace a larger purpose, the new CEO began to optimize operations. He optimized and optimized. The business saw some incremental gains. Then growth flattened. And then eventually declined.

At some point, operational optimization meets the law of diminishing returns.

For this company's prospects, there is nothing to believe in. Nothing to rally around. All the maneuvers and functional optimization ended up having the exact opposite effect than what was intended. It has no belongingness and no purpose. So it flounders. Its story is a cautionary tale for any brand that dismisses the importance of creating a sense of belonging.

There is huge opportunity to fulfill the need for belonging in a way that helps people feel like, by belonging, they are making a profound difference for those around them. By inviting people into our Big Audacious Meaning, we not only connect with our believers' need to belong, but we also fulfill their desire to create meaning in their lives – that unmatched feeling that our days mean something and that what we do can have an impact on our world.

Goodbye brand fan. Hello brand collaborator.

For years, brands have wanted us to become their fans. Beyond just buying their products and services, they have wanted us to advocate for them. In fact, the measure of this is the Net Promoter Score – a tool that measures our willingness to recommend a brand to others.

Companies work to gain high Net Promoter Scores. They

may take the tack of providing outstanding value. Others may try to capture a certain zeitgeist that people are drawn to (hoping we will wear their logos.) They want us to become that fan.

The thing is, this language feels out of step with today's sensibility. The word 'fan' suggest someone who is passive. It's a person who sits on the sideline. Not really engaging, but rather, cheering on whoever it is they align with. Yet, that's how the majority of brands treat us.

The trouble with this is that it feels like a one-way street. If we advocate for them, what do we get in return? Maybe recommending their brand reflects well upon us. Maybe, by displaying their logo, we get to be part of the image that they have created with their brand. But the fact is, none of us wants to sit on the sidelines. We want to be participants.

When we step back and examine it, it feels like the brand is requesting a lot from this relationship.

What if we felt like we had a bigger role? What if there was something beyond just being a promoter? There would have to be a way to engage with the brand that goes beyond just connecting. It would have to feel more like a partnership that we have with that brand. There would have to be an opportunity to become a collaborator with that brand.

That is a tall order. It's going to take more than offering the features and benefits of whatever product or service we create. It's even going to take more than creating a desirable image. This requires that the brand commit to something beyond itself. Something that can have a real and meaningful impact for people. A brand that commits to this creates a unique opportunity for all of its potential believers to join in as collaborators. To be part of what feels a lot like a movement.

In this scenario, it's no longer just about why we should buy from a brand. Our purchasing decision becomes a lever to help us do more than acquire goods and services. It becomes a means to accomplish a larger purpose. This creates a very different relationship between the brand and us. As collaborators on this larger purpose, we begin to feel more like a peer. We begin to feel like we have skin in the game in creating this change in the world. If we feel that we have skin in the game, it's going to increase loyalty. We want to see our decisions and actions build upon each other as we work with the brand to pursue that Big Audacious Meaning. As collaborators, the relationship is no longer dominated by a transaction. Rather, it is based on something we believe in and actively champion. Now when we wear a company logo, it's not just because we align with an idea that the company promotes. We wear it because we feel like we are actively involved in contributing to a positive change in the world.

Igniting hope

For all team members, hope is a powerful motivator. In the face of the most difficult challenges, it is the hope that springs from purpose that helps us push through. It's the belief that our good and honorable effort will lead us to a better place. It inspires all of us to not only give our time to an effort, but our hearts as well.

For all those we serve, hope is an irresistible force. It helps us imagine a future inhabited by the best of us. And it helps us feel like we can be part of something greater than ourselves in the pursuit of that purpose.

We live in a cynical, narcissistic world. One filled to the brim with attention-deficit-fueled fake news and disposable amusement. It's easy to get overwhelmed. Or worse, just beaten down. We need the hope that comes from a purpose. We need to be able to look forward to the things we can do to make a difference in a life, community, and even the world.

Key Takeaways

- Everything should be built on an undeniable and irresistible sense of purpose. It should be demonstrated in what the organization says and what it does.

- After we clarify our purpose, we have to ensure our people are true believers. We do that by using our anthem to make the unveiling a big deal. And then by creating a sustained effort to demonstrate the importance of our purpose.

- A Big Audacious Meaning creates a connectedness where our believers feel like they are pursuing something with us that can make a real difference in the world.

- As collaborators, our believers' relationship with the brand is no longer dominated by the transaction. Now when they wear a company logo, it's because they feel like they are actively involved in contributing to a positive change in the world.

- Today, we need the hope that comes from a purpose. We need to be able to look forward to the things we can do to make a difference in a life, community, and even the world.

SECTION 6: UNLEASHING OUR PURPOSE-DRIVEN STORY

You know that feeling. We read our organization's website and something just feels off. Maybe it's obvious that the message is a murky mess. More often than not, it's not that bad. It's serviceable. But it just leaves us feeling flat. Or just not feeling anything at all.

Our story is one of the greatest assets we have. It holds the potential to carry our Big Audacious Meaning out into the world. To engage, delight, inspire, and more. Those are incredible experiences that we have the potential to create. They are experiences that all us humans crave. In fact, we'll go out of our way to find those organizations that can engage, delight, and inspire us. And we will reward them for helping us be part of something that satisfies these desires to feel extraordinary things.

When we consider that, it's downright baffling that organizations will settle for a serviceable story.

Purpose-driven brands range from retail operations to business-to-business firms to non-profits. As different as they are, they share a trait that gets unlocked when a brand commits to clarifying that purpose. They discover the ability to tell powerful stories. Stories of the quest. Stories of those who have been inspired to join in. Stories of the difference the organization is making.

We humans love stories. Not just because they entertain. That's important, but there's more. Stories humanize information. Think about the times we have tried to explain a complex subject to someone. To speed understanding, we'll put the information in some sort of context. We'll say, "It's like this…" And then we'll tell a story. Either a real-life example or something we invent in order to illustrate our point.

These are not sales pitches (although they have an incredible power to move business). They connect with people in a way that surpasses any sales pitch or list of features and benefits. They get people to care. And when people care, they have potential to become more than customers. They suddenly have the potential to become our evangelists.

I worked with one medical device business owner who was struggling to elevate his brand above the low-cost providers and slap-dash-solution competitors. It would have been very easy just to ask, "So, what makes you different?" We would have gotten to some explanation of why his offering was a few degrees better in this or that regard. Maybe we would have illustrated why his features were better than those other guys. That would have been fine. And may have even resulted in some marginal success. But that wasn't the question that needed asking. That questions was, "Why do you care." That one query unleashed a flood of stories. He told of the incredible difference his company had made in the lives of those they helped. He told stories about people discovering a new lease on life. Stories of relationships restored. It was absolutely captivating. More importantly, we started to uncover that incredible purpose that drove him (and his brand). That's what needed to be brought forward. That was the thing that would elevate and propel his business. The stories were there just waiting to be unlocked. They weren't stories about features and benefits. They were stories about a purpose.

Stories have the power to do some remarkable things for our Big Audacious Meaning. To begin with, they remove any vagueness in the expression of our purpose. A purpose is expressed in big and bold ways. That's the magic of it. When we tell stories that illustrate the purpose, it becomes real and specific. It becomes concrete.

Stories are emotional. We forget statistics. But we remember how we felt when we heard the story. That is what makes it unforgettable.

Most of all, stories are human. When we see how a purpose makes a profound difference for another person, the idea is no longer just a lofty thought. It becomes about a person who we can empathize with. And because of that, it connects with us.

A Big Audacious Meaning is one of the most fundamental and powerful ideas any organization can adopt. When done right, it is impressive and inspiring. Add in storytelling and it becomes concrete, emotional, and relatable. All the things that make a purpose unforgettable.

CHAPTER 12
Transforming our story's strategic foundation

In today's world, it's very rare for an offering to have functional differentiation. That's when we have a clearly differentiating feature that the other guys don't have.

A few decades ago, it was easier. You may have been able to introduce a feature or a process that was unique, and then capitalize on it while the competition tried to catch up. Today, technology has made it too easy for a competitor to spin up a similar offer at record speed. Or for entirely new competitors to start up.

Technology has been the great leveler. It has increased anyone's ability to turbo boost their speed to market. And it has reduced the cost barriers to getting into business or launching a new line of business.

There is a real danger here. If anyone can launch a competing offer and there is no significant differentiation that's readily apparent to the prospect, a scary thing happens. We find ourselves suddenly having to compete largely on price. Oh, a few other factors may come into play, like service. But if the primary factor is the price, we'll find ourselves in a race to the bottom, as our once unique offering becomes another me-too option in a commodity market.

That sucks. But that's the reality. Differentiating a brand today is tough.

Yet within this reality, we still see organizations relying

on a strategic thinking process bent on defining functional differentiation. Do we believe that if we just think a little harder we can bring back the days when functional differentiation was enough?

Maybe it's time to think a little differently.

Focusing on a different kind of difference

It's interesting to look at what brand stories have become today. Companies now quibble with competitors over mere degrees of differentiation. In order to make a case, the brand stories become complicated as they attempt to portray the fine distinctions that they are trying to own. As the stories become more complicated, any chance of capturing something that will inspire people goes out the window. Ultimately, we all become less likely to pay attention.

If we're relying on a story that is not clearly unique, powerfully simple, and inspiring, then we are just adding to the ocean of white noise out there.

So what is an organization to do? Will it become a game of who can exploit the latest technology the fastest? With today's ever-increasing pace of change, that sounds like a hamster wheel from hell.

It's no longer enough to talk about our attributes (our widget is 40% faster!) and functional benefits (our faster widgets help you get more done!) Simon Sinek helps illustrate this, "...we rationalize based on more tangible factors, like the design or the service or the brand. This is the basis for the false assumption that price or features matter more than they do. Those things matter, they provide us the tangible things we can point to rationalize our decision-making, but they don't set the course and they don't inspire behavior."[49]

We're going to have to get to something more meaningful for our prospects. I'm talking about building a story on a purpose you embrace. That's something that has a profound effect. Something that can cause our prospects to willingly lower the barriers they put up and allow us to enter that magical realm of consideration.

Imagine no longer quibbling with competitors over whose attribute or functional benefit is marginally better. Imagine, instead, telling our prospects how they can be part of something that makes the world around us a little bit better place.

To do this, we need to ask, "Is our big question, 'What makes us different?' Or, is it, 'What difference will we make?'"

Creating a real reason to care

Think about why people engage with us. I'll go one better here. Let's ask our clients/customers. I'm going to guess we're not going to hear things like, "I'm particularly enthralled with their 7-point inspection plan."

No, we're more likely to hear, "I trust them." Or, "They understand what's important to me."

We may have a feature that we are particularly proud of. It may even be clearly superior to the closest competitor. We fixate on these things. When we step back and look at it through the half-interested eyes of our prospect, we realize that the difference is rarely the game changer that we think it is.

Most often, we stake our claims of differentiation around our unique combination of rational attributes. This could be features as well as processes. This 'secret sauce' becomes the centerpiece of how we tell our story.

This is rarely as compelling as we had hoped. And for good reason. Since we're talking about a combination of attributes, it becomes significantly more difficult to explain in a simple and memorable way. That's why it's rare for this secret sauce to pack the emotional punch we desire.

I have done a lot of work with financial services organizations. If there ever was an industry where parity runs rampant, it's this one. I was working with a bank that had an offering that suffered from this parity.

We went through the strategic exercises. We found a few features that were worth mentioning (functional attributes) and put them together in a mix that achieved a small level of differentiation. We could have stopped there. But we knew we weren't going to move anybody. We needed to find that big thing that would inspire people. We needed to rethink the offering.

We recommended a reconfiguration that would allow us to show prospects how the offering could help them work toward a life they aspired to. It could be in big ways – making big strides and fulfilling big dreams. But it didn't have to be that. It could be small steps that could lead someone to getting out of debt.

We asked, "What if we could build solutions that allow people to take control and design a life that fits their needs, ultimately giving them incredible confidence." Think about the difference that can make for them. Think about how much happier it could make someone feel.

It wasn't just wishful thinking. It is an idea that was founded in a purpose of helping people have a better relationship with their money. An idea that could make a real difference in their lives. In short, we stopped trying to tell prospects how awesome our offering was and started showing them how awesome they could feel.

We immediately talked about how exciting it would be for the front line people. We could imagine them being able to sit across from a prospect and tell them how they could help that person along the path to the life that the prospect wanted to create. Think about how much more profound that is than talking about the features of the account or the rewards that the person could earn. Think about how compelling that would be if you were that prospect.

We couldn't have gotten there without thinking about the rational side of things. But we also recognized that that's not where the magic happens. When we let a purpose take the lead, we found it less important to compare ourselves to others. In fact, we found ourselves talking less about ourselves and more about those that we desired to inspire and help.

Purpose is the new positioning

I have a friend who I have enjoyed working with over the years. He's a smart marketer with a healthy cynicism – a valued trait for refining positioning. A healthy cynicism has shown to improve the ability to question the validity of positioning assumptions.

We have worked on a number of projects together. We have shared a great give and take when it comes to debating the mechanics of the positioning for different brands.

Like other good marketers, we have worked diligently to fashion and refine positioning statements for each project we have tackled.

I look back on these efforts and I have mixed feelings. I have enjoyed working with my friend. And the positioning was rationally sound – well thought out and thoroughly vetted. The work that resulted from the effort was solid. I wanted it to be inspiring. But, I can't say it got to that. It was simply solid.

We had well-made positioning. But something was missing.

In 1981, Jack Trout and Al Ries gave us the book *Positioning: The Battle For Your Mind*. It introduced the idea of owning a position in the mind of your prospect.

These positioning exercises are rational endeavors. We start with a standard framework, then fill in the blanks until we have a completed statement. Here's an example of a typical positioning statement structure:

For (THE INDIVIDUALS WE HOPE TO SERVE) Who are looking for (THEIR UNMET NEED) Our organization (THE SUMMATION OF WHAT WE DO THAT MEETS THAT UNMET NEED) Unlike (COMPETITIVE ALTERNATIVES) Ours is the only organization that offers (FUNCTIONAL ATTRIBUTES) That deliver (EMOTIONAL BENEFIT)

For over three decades, we identified the functional attributes that led us to the emotional benefit. This exercise would help us carve out that position that would be ownable and defendable.

Over those decades, a funny thing happened. It became more and more challenging to define a position that was significantly different. Today, it seems the differences are measured in mere degrees.

There is another challenge we face when working with positioning. It's subtly deceptive.

It's easy to believe we are creating real and meaningful differentiation. It's all about finding the valued attributes of a brand. Defining how that combination of attributes differs from all the other competitive offerings. Identifying the emotional benefit. And documenting how all these elements come together to carve out a unique position in the minds of prospects.

Through this process, we rationally build the case for our brands. I have to admit that I love the process. There is something satisfying about systematically building and honing a positioning statement.

But, we can get so involved in debating the intricacies and filling in the blanks that we forget to step back and ask, "Will anybody really care about all this?"

I experienced this very situation with my friend and marketing colleague. As we got deeper and deeper into the process, we were less likely to question whether we were defining something that had a significant enough difference to really be compelling to a prospect. We were simply working with what we had. And we were excited about completing the process.

Did we create differentiation? Technically, yes. Emotionally? Not so much. Which explains why the work that came out of that position was solid, but not necessarily inspiring.

What's the purpose?

I think about the question, "What's the purpose?" It's often used as an expression of exasperation. Like saying, "There is no meaning to what we are doing." Maybe we should be asking it in just that manner when we are faced with developing the new positioning of a brand.

Then, we should follow it with the more literal interpretation of the question. To ask, "What is the Big Audacious Meaning our brand can serve?"

Shifting our focus to purpose is exponentially more powerful. We are no longer quibbling with our competitors about why we are a few degrees better. Instead, we are creating a movement to improve life for those we serve. And we're inviting everyone along to help amplify the efforts. Even our competitors.

That's a radical shift from the way we have been thinking about creating differentiation for more than 30 years.

I think about that title from the book by Trout and Ries from 1981: *Positioning: The Battle For Your Mind.* And I think about the evolution we have gone through since that time. The realization I keep coming back to is that it is no longer enough to create positioning that wins the battle for the mind. Research from the fields of behavioral economics to neuroscience has shown us that that's not where the real victory is won.

If we want differentiation that is meaningful, compelling, and inspiring, then we need to turn our attention to where decisions are made. Trust is forged. And evangelism is sparked. We need to win the heart.

Key Takeaways

- In today's world, it's very rare for an offering to have functional differentiation. Technology has made it too easy for a competitor to spin up a similar offer at record speed. Or for entirely new competitors to start up.

- Most often, we stake our claims of differentiation around our unique combination of rational attributes. This 'secret sauce' becomes how we tell our story. Unfortunately, it becomes significantly more difficult to explain in a simple and memorable way.

- If we're relying on a story that is not clearly unique, powerfully simple, and inspiring, then we are just adding to the ocean of white noise out there.

- When we let a purpose take the lead, we find it less important to compare ourselves to others. We need to change the question from, "What makes us different?" to "What difference will we make?"

- It is no longer enough to create positioning that wins the battle for the mind. We need to win the heart. Purpose is the new positioning.

CHAPTER 13
The Thrust Story Framework

Clarifying a Big Audacious Meaning is a significant step for the organization. It's not unusual that it creates a sense of urgency for us to incorporate it into our story so we can begin to take our purpose to the world. In order to do that, we need to set out a structure that will help define how it comes to life in the story that our organization tells.

Traditionally, that was done through a positioning statement structure that we previously discussed. Here is that structure:

For (THE INDIVIDUALS WE HOPE TO SERVE)

Who are looking for (THEIR UNMET NEED)

Our organization (THE SUMMATION OF WHAT WE DO THAT MEETS THAT UNMET NEED)

Unlike (COMPETITIVE ALTERNATIVES)

Ours is the only organization that offers (FUNCTIONAL ATTRIBUTES)

That deliver (EMOTIONAL BENEFIT)

While this is a very functional form, it misses the bigger opportunity (you'll notice that the idea of a Big Audacious Meaning is not present.) We all want to make sure the stories that we tell are taking full advantage of the potential they hold to move and inspire those that we hope to serve. In order to do that, we need a structure that's proven to unlock that potential.

So many of the stories that we know and love have such a structure. It applies to everything from ancient mythology to modern movies. Joseph Campbell defined the structure in what he calls the Hero's Journey from his 1949 book, *The Hero with a Thousand Faces*. He summarized it this way, "A hero ventures forth from the world of common day into a region of supernatural wonder: fabulous forces are there encountered and a decisive victory is won: the hero comes back from this mysterious adventure with the power to bestow boons on his fellow man."[50]

While we won't use the 17 stages of the hero's journey that Campbell outlines, it is worth pulling out the major components from his summarization:

- The Hero

- The Villain

- The Sage Guide

- The False Paths

- The Discoveries

- The Triumph

- The Transformation

Using these components, we create the Thrust Story Framework. Here is how that structure comes to life.

There is a **HERO**.

And this hero has a **VILLAIN**.

To defeat this villain, our hero embarks on a quest led by a **SAGE GUIDE**

This sage guide helps our hero avoid **THE FALSE PATHS**.

And assists our hero in experiencing **THE DISCOVERIES** along the way.

All of this helps our hero **TRIUMPH** over the villain.

And, ultimately, experience **THE TRANSFORMATION**

This structure takes the best of the positioning structure, places it in a much more compelling storytelling structure, and adds the unparalleled impact of our Big Audacious Meaning.

Here is a breakdown of the major components:

- **THE HERO**

  Who is the Hero of this story we are creating? Is it our organization? After all, it is the story we are creating. We should be the Hero of our story, right? This is where a shockingly large number of organizations go wrong. How many times have we encountered an organization intent on telling us the saga of who they are, what they do, and why they're special? It's as if they believe that the telling of their triumphs will mesmerize us. Let's be honest. Nobody wants to listen to that. We want to be swept up into something that invites us to imagine ourselves inside the narrative. Something that captures our desires and absolutely captivates us. That's not the story of what the organization does or how it does it, or even why it thinks it's special. Before we begin any story, we should go to the beginning of our Thrust Story Framework. There, before anything else, is the answer to the question, "Who is our Hero?" It is the individuals we hope to serve. When we make them the hero, we create a very different story from the inward-focused, self-serving tale too many organizations tell.

• THE VILLAIN

In a positioning statement, it's called the unmet need. But it is much more powerful (and fun) to think of it as the Villain. The Villain is the thing that our Hero must overcome. As such, it is the thing that pushes our Hero out of the comfort zone, sending him or her on a quest. A Villain can be external – something that stands in the way of our Hero experiencing the triumph. For example, it could be a rash of overdraft fees that our Hero can't seem to escape each month. This is a Villain that causes frustration and stops our Hero from being able to build savings. A Villain can also be internal. Maybe it's a lack of confidence that keeps our Hero from seeking a better job or pursuing a degree. Everyone has Villains in their life. They can be keeping us from solving a problem or taking advantage of an opportunity.

- ## THE SAGE GUIDE

  This is where our organization comes into the story. We are the Sage Guide that will help our Hero on his or her quest. We need to first help our hero understand why we deserve this role. We do this by demonstrating why we are uniquely qualified. This can be through our expertise, our tools, and more. In the positioning statement, this is described as how we meet the unmet need (which is rather uninspiring). Characterizing ourselves as the Sage Guide gives us the ability to paint an expressive picture of why we are unique.

- ## THE FALSE PATHS

  There are multiple paths our hero can take in the quest to overcome the Villain. As his or her sage guide, we know there is one true path (the one we provide!) The False Paths are our competitors (labeled as the competitive alternatives in the positioning statement). As that trusted guide, we must help our Hero understand why those other routes do not hold the potential that our path offers.

- ## THE DISCOVERIES

  The Discoveries are those special things that our Hero will experience through the quest that help him or her overcome the Villain. In the positioning statement, these are referred to as our functional attributes. These are three or so of our attributes that demonstrate our uniqueness and superiority when compared to the False Paths (competitors). For a checking account product I helped a bank take to market, these attributes included the highest interest rate in town, no ATM fees, and a unique program that helped customers learn how to do more with their money.

- **THE TRIUMPH**

How does our Hero win? Can we help him or her imagine what life would be like when that happens? In the positioning statement, we characterize this as the emotional benefit. This points us to that idealized end to the Hero's quest. The conquering of the Villain. It captures how our Hero will feel. More importantly, it offers the elusive enlightenment that all our Heroes seek. That is powerful. We need to make sure the language we use here does not underplay the magnitude of this Triumph. It should do everything it can to lift up and amplify our Hero's newfound sense of hope.

- **THE TRANSFORMATION**

The Triumph is not the end. We can offer something that shows how our Hero's triumph can translate into a greater good that spreads into the world. This game-changing idea is our Big Audacious Meaning. This is an idea that is inspiring and irresistible in the possibilities that it ignites in our Hero's imagination. After all, this is how we will help our Heroes be part of something larger than themselves. Something that can make a profound difference in a life, a community, or even the world. This is the element that elevates the story. It is what takes it to an epic level. It will transform our stories just as it transforms our Heroes.

Here is an example of how the Thrust Story Framework works using First Federal Bank's story:

> **THE HERO**: There is a woman with a young family
>
> **THE VILLAIN**: who feels like she is constantly struggling with getting her money to help her do more.
>
> **THE SAGE GUIDE**: This sends her on a search, where she discovers someone who she can lean on to help her build a better financial future - First Federal.
>
> **THE FALSE PATHS**: She resists being sucked into the behemoth nationwide banks where she would be lost and forgotten. And escapes the generic community banks that could little to help her overcome her villain.
>
> **THE DISCOVERIES**: Instead she follows a path that leads her to an enchanting combination that includes the most rewarding checking account in the city, servant-hearted people who can help her make sense of it all, and a unique program that promotes

stronger communities by helping people discover how to take control of their money.

THE TRIUMPH: This allows her to overcome the struggle and find an unmatched sense of financial wellbeing.

THE TRANSFORMATION: Most of all, she feels like she is part of something special - part of a movement where people, organizations, and communities can all prosper together.

With the organizations I have worked with, I have noticed an interesting thing that happens when we introduce the Big Audacious Meaning into the equation. It changes how we fill in all areas of the framework. The Hero becomes nobler. The Villain becomes more pronounced. We assign greater value to ourselves (The Sage Guide) and The Discoveries in light of this larger purpose. We begin to see how this distinctly separates us from The False Paths. And leads to The Triumph, which feels more valuable. Ultimately, it helps our heroes feel like they can take part in a Transformation by making a difference in our world.

The result of all this is that we develop a story framework that is deeper and more resonant than anything we have had before.

The first step

Everything we do should begin with the individual. The customer. The prospect. The constituent. However we want to portray it. Our story must be irresistible to these potential believers. So we must begin by having exceptional clarity about them. Who they are. How they think. Their needs. Their wants. Their hopes and desires. They are the groups of people that our Big Audacious Meaning serves. They are the ones we aim to help and to inspire.

Only by understanding these individuals can we craft something that will have a profound impact on them. This is why we must understand these groups of people (segments) and create personas of for each of them.

We start with any data that the organization may have aggregated. This can come from sales reports, website analytics, customer intercept research and more. We're looking for the quantifiable data. This can be augmented with industry research. Many times, our trade organizations may conduct original quantitative and qualitative studies. There may even be research generated by other trusted third party sources such as universities. Bringing all of this together gives us insight into who they are.

Next, we consult with our marketing and sales leadership to get their point of view. It's important that we get the perspective from both of these disciplines.

While it is important to get the leadership's point of view, we must talk to the frontline people as well. These are our organization's representatives who have a direct connection to the different prospects on a daily basis. I have found that it is these folks who can offer the surprising insight and unique point of view that only comes from having this constant close contact with those we hope to serve.

This qualitative research helps us understand more about the individual's attitudes and behaviors. These are the insights that don't appear in the numbers of the quantitative research. But, sometimes, can help us explain why the numbers are the way they are. And even where the numbers might be headed.

We need both views of those we hope to serve. Together, they help us round out the picture, giving us a view of who they are and how they think and act. With this investigation complete, we can move on to creating personas.

Personas bring our individuals to life, by creating a profile of each. A great persona makes that profile seem like a living, breathing person. It gives her or him a name. It could define a demographic profile, including things like age, education, household income, family status, and more. It also documents how this person thinks, describing his or her challenges, needs, wants, and desires. And the persona describes how this person acts.

By the end of the persona process, we have a group of interesting stories. Each is about an individual who is representative of one of our segments. It is important that we talk about these individuals in a very human manner – as if we were describing those we know very well. If our story is to have a profound impact on a life, then we need to have incredible empathy for that life. Well-crafted personas help create that empathy.

Key Takeaways

- Joseph Campbell gave us a definitive storytelling structure in what he calls the Hero's Journey from his 1949 book, *The Hero with a Thousand Faces*. We distill Campbell's 17 stages down to 7 components: The Hero, The Villain, The Sage Guide, The False Paths, The Discoveries, The Triumph, and The Transformation. Using these components, we create the Thrust Story Framework.

- When we introduce the Big Audacious Meaning (The Transformation) into the equation, it changes how we fill in all areas of the framework, making it more resonant than anything we have had before.

- Everything we do should begin with the individual. This is why we must understand these groups of people (segments) and create personas of for each of them.

- By the end of the persona process, we have a group of interesting stories. Each is about an individual who is representative of one of our segments.

CHAPTER 14
The Thrust Story Framework workshop

With our personas built, we can move on to creating a story framework for each. We should have an easel pad sheet for each persona. On the sheet, put the name of the persona at the top. Below the persona name, list out each part of the story framework:

There is a _____

(A description of our Hero.)

And this hero _____

(A description of the Villain – the challenge our Hero faces.)

Our Hero embarks on a quest led by _____

(A description of us as their Sage Guide.)

This Sage Guide helps our Hero _____

(A description of how we as a Sage Guide help our
Hero avoid the False Paths.)

And assists our Hero in experiencing _____

(A description of The Discoveries our Hero
experiences.)

All of this helps our Hero _____

(A description of how our Hero Triumphs over the
Villain.)

And, ultimately, experiences _____

(A description of The Transformation our hero
experiences.)

In the workshop, we'll collaborate as a group to fill in each
part of the Thrust Story Framework for each of our personas.

- The Hero – We will reference the persona that we
  created for this Hero. This is just a broad brush.
  Going back to the First Federal Bank example we
  characterized the Hero this way – "There is a woman
  with a young family..."

- The Villain – We go back to the persona we created for a description of The Villain. This is the problem or the opportunity that The Hero is trying to address. In the First Federal Bank example, we said, "…who feels like she is constantly struggling with getting her money to help her do more."

- The Sage Guide – In this section we summarize, why we are uniquely qualified to help our Hero fight that Villain. In the First Federal Bank example, we said, "This sends her on a search, where she discovers someone who she can lean on to help her build a better financial future - First Federal."

- The False Paths – We summarize the top competitive alternatives and why they are insufficient compared to our solution. In the First Federal Bank example, we said, "She resists being sucked into the behemoth nationwide banks where she would be lost and forgotten. And escapes the generic community banks that could little to help her overcome her villain."

- The Discoveries – The discoveries are our functional attributes. These are the three or so things that we offer or do that provide proof to The Triumph (benefit) that our Hero will experience. In the First Federal Bank example, we said, "Instead she follows a path that leads her to an enchanting combination that includes the most rewarding checking account in the city, servant-hearted people who can help her makes sense of it all, and a unique program that promotes stronger communities by helping people discover how to take control of their money."

- The Triumph – This is the emotional benefit that our Hero feels after experiencing The Discoveries. In the First Federal Bank example, we said, "This allows her to overcome the struggle and find an unmatched sense of financial wellbeing."

- The Transformation – Our story structure is capped off with the most important element – The Transformation (our Big Audacious Meaning). We have already defined this. Simply fill it in on the sheet. As a reminder of how that fits with the rest of the story structure, here is what we said for First Federal Bank, "Most of all, she feels like she is part of something special - part of a movement where people, organizations, and communities can all prosper together."

The Characteristic Spectrums

While we have our stakeholders together, we will want them to help us define our voice. This helps ensure that our stories sound true to who we are. In order to accomplish this, we will create Characteristic Spectrums. Imagine a slider. On the far left hand side is the word 'Serious'. On the far right hand side is the word 'Humorous'. There is a bar connecting the two. And on that bar is a slider that can be positioned on one end or the other or anywhere in between. Where would we place that slider to describe our brand personality? This is a much more nuanced approach as opposed to just picking a set of characteristics. After all, it's not likely that we can describe a brand as totally serious or completely humorous. It is more likely to be degrees somewhere between the two. This is why the slider gives us a truer representation of the characteristic of the brand personality.

One word of warning. As we pair up characteristics, let's make sure each is potentially desirable. For example, I've seen spectrums where at one end is the word 'Warm' and at the other end is the word 'Cold'. Or at one end is 'Simple' and at the other end is 'Complicated'. Do you know of any brand that would consider 'Cold' and 'Complicated' as potential characteristics?

Choose the pairings thoughtfully. The juxtaposition should help illustrate the nuance of our characteristics. Here is an example of meaningful pairings:

Rational <-----> Emotional

Informative <-----> Inspiring

Expert <-----> Peer

Serious <-----> Humorous

Objective <-----> Persuasive

Mature <-----> Youthful

Traditional <-----> Non-traditional

Pragmatic <-----> Idealistic

Conventional <-----> Unconventional

Cosmopolitan <-----> Folksy

Customize the spectrum to capture characteristics specific to the organization. Then, list the characteristic spectrums on an easel pad sheet. During the workshop, we'll ask the participants to place a sticker on each spectrum. For example, look at the first one I listed:

Rational <-----> Emotional

Each participant would determine where the organization falls along this spectrum by placing his or her sticker at that point.

At the end of this exercise, we can summarize the votes for all the characteristics and document the personality of the organization.

Prepping the participants

As with our Big Audacious Meaning workshop, it is important to prepare our participants. This ensures that all those who are participating know our objective, understand what we will be doing, and have a good idea of what is required of them.

Prepare an overview presentation that shows how we will be building the Thrust Story Framework. Detail all the areas we will be addressing and describe what we will be looking for. Also, let them know that we will be defining the brand characteristics as well. This presentation can be delivered via a webinar to make it easier to coordinate all the attendees. It can usually be completed in a half hour.

Don't be tempted to skip this precursor to the workshop. It is an important component that can help create more receptive and engaged participants. And, help eliminate a lot of explaining during the workshop, allowing more time for productive debate and ideation.

The workshop

The workshop is where it all comes together. It is the culmination of some great discovery and thoughtful input. This should be a time of anticipation and excitement. We have prepared our insight. We have prepared our participants. Now it's time to build that sturdy framework that will support our compelling story. And to confirm the Characteristics Spectrums that will define our personality.

It is important to set expectations for our participants from the beginning of the session. We are not looking for perfect prose here. We are looking to narrow in on the strongest ideas and make sure they work together in our Thrust Story Framework. There will be time later to refine the language.

During the workshop, we'll go through each of our easel pad sheets that we have created. By the end of the workshop, we will have the framework of our story structures.

When we fill in the last blank of the story structure statement sheet, we should take a step back and do a gut check. Have we truly defined The Villain? Have we proven that we are their Sage Guide? Does our combination of The Discoveries provide compelling proof? And are we delivering The Triumph that is exceptionally moving? Finally, does it all roll up to irrefutably support The Transformation – our Big Audacious Meaning? If we're unsure about any of this, we need to discuss and adjust as a group. This is the time for us to push each other. The ideas here are crucial. We can't settle for "good enough".

There should be a great sense of accomplishment at the end of this session. We will have built that sturdy framework for our story. And defined the personality that will help bring it to life.

Now it's time to refine the language and begin to create our purpose-driven story.

Key Takeaways

- In the workshop, we'll collaborate as a group to fill in each part of the Thrust Story Framework for each of our personas.

- Our stakeholders will also help us define our voice. This helps ensure that our stories sound true to who we are. In order to accomplish this, we will create Characteristic Spectrums.

- As with our Big Audacious Meaning workshop, it is important to prepare our participants. This ensures that all those who are participating know our objective, understand what we will be doing, and have a good idea of what is required of them.

- In the workshop, we are looking to narrow in on the strongest ideas and make sure they work together in our Thrust Story Framework. There will be time later to refine the language.

CHAPTER 15
Building our purpose-driven story

The Thrust Story Framework we just outlined gives us the makings of an epic tale. Here's the really great part. These components can be organized in a myriad of ways, allowing us to tailor our stories to wherever our prospects are in their journey to becoming our customers.

To illustrate this idea, let's look at the customer journey. It defines the 6 stages we all go through in our engagement with any organization. Here are those 6 stages and the question we ask at each:

- Define - What is the challenge or opportunity that I'm trying to address?

- Discover - How do I address this challenge or opportunity?

- Evaluate - Can I compare options available to me?

- Decide - How do I validate that this is the right solution for me?

- Review - Was this a good decision?

- Advocate - Shouldn't others know about this?

The question our prospects have at the Define stage is quite different than the question they have at the Decision stage. So the answer that we give – the story we tell – is quite different at each of these stages as well. Before we freak out about having to write 6 different stories, remember that all the components are the same from story to story. It is how we order them and the time we spend on each that makes each story unique. This makes it all less overwhelming. Let's take a look at how we structure our story for each stage of the journey. For a visual representation of the story framework at each stage of the journey, check out the Thrust Story Composition at dansalva.com/resources.

Define

At this stage, they are asking, "What is the challenge or opportunity that I'm trying to address?" So it is only natural that we start with *THE VILLAIN*. This sets the stage by empathizing with the struggle they have. We will follow it by showing them that they can find the help they need with us as their *SAGE GUIDE*. And we'll introduce them to *THE DISCOVERIES* they'll make along the way that leads them to *THE TRIUMPH*, and ultimately, *THE TRANSFORMATION*.

Here is how much of this story we dedicate to each component:

- **30% of the story:** *THE VILLAIN* – we have the ability to build a connection by demonstrating our empathy with their plight

- **5% of the story:** *THE SAGE GUIDE* – we will briefly touch on how we can help them defeat that Villain.

- **5% of the story:** *THE DISCOVERIES*– we also

briefly touch on The Discoveries that will help along their way.

- **20% of the story:** *THE TRIUMPH–* we want them to get a sense of what can be gained, but move quickly to the bigger inspiration of our Big Audacious Meaning

- **40% of our story:** *THE TRANSFORMATION –* this is the time to inspire our prospects, so our Big Audacious Meaning gets the spotlight

Discover

At the Discover stage, the question is, "How do I address this challenge or opportunity?" Here it makes sense to start with *THE TRIUMPH*. Remember, our prospects aren't looking at specific organizations yet to help them. Focusing on the emotional benefit first allows them to imagine how they will feel once they slay the dragon that is *THE VILLAIN*. This also creates a natural bridge to *THE TRANSFORMATION*, which builds on the impact of *THE TRIUMPH* by tapping into their deepest desires. We will let them know how we can be their *SAGE GUIDE* and *THE DISCOVERIES* they will make, but the story at this stage is less about what we do and more about how they can feel.

Here is how much of this story we dedicate to each component:

- **30% of the story:** *THE TRIUMPH –* we want them to feel like there is something bigger to be gained.

- **20% of the story:** *THE VILLAIN –* we don't overplay the struggle here. It's more important to use it as context to help them feel that what they can accomplish is significant.

- **30% of our story:** *THE TRANSFORMATION* – this helps keep the emotional energy high, helping them feel like this journey is worthwhile.

- **10% of the story:** *THE SAGE GUIDE* – we will remind them that we are a helpful ally in their quest.

- **10% of the story:** *THE DISCOVERIES*– we also touch on those functional attributes that will help them in their quest.

Evaluate

At this stage, they are asking, "Can I compare options available to me?" This is where we want to lead with how we can be their *SAGE GUIDE* and *THE DISCOVERIES* they'll make along the way. This is how we stack up against the competition. Which is a good reason to also talk about *THE FALSE PATHS* that they'll want to avoid. And we'll highlight *THE TRIUMPH* that flows out of what we do and how we do it. And of course, all this should point to *THE TRANSFORMATION*. We include a mention of *THE* VILLAIN here as well, allowing us to illustrate how efficiently we meet that need with everything we can offer.

Here is how much of this story we dedicate to each component:

- **10% of the story:** *THE SAGE GUIDE* – we want to remind our Hero that we have the unique help that they seek.

- **50% of the story:** *THE DISCOVERIES* – this is

the time to really illustrate the details of our unique help so our Hero can make their evaluation and feel confident in choosing us.

- **20% of the story:** *THE TRIUMPH* – this stage is more about the details, but we need to punctuate those details with the benefit in order to keep them charged up.

- **10% of our story:** *THE TRANSFORMATION* – this may be a stage where they are weighing more rational elements, but adding the flavor of our Big Audacious Meaning can make those rational pieces feel just a little more special

- **10% of the story:** *THE VILLAIN* – they are at a part of the journey where spending too much time on The Villain could feel unnecessary. We can remind them of the challenge, but then we need to move on.

Decide

At the Decide stage, the question they are asking is, "How do I validate that this is the right solution for me?" In answering, we want to lead with *THE TRIUMPH* and *THE TRANSFORMATION*. These two are the engaging and emotional components that will help cement the decision of our prospects to become our customers. We will spend less time on how we are *THE SAGE GUIDE* and *THE DISCOVERIES* since these were examined and weighed in the last stage. Additionally, we may remind them of *THE VILLAIN*, but we won't spend much time on it.

Here is how much of this story we dedicate to each component:

- **40% of our story:** *THE TRANSFORMATION* – we know that the decision-making function resides in the emotional part of the brain, so we want to bring this component forward. Nothing is more emotionally powerful than our Big Audacious Meaning.

- **30% of the story:** *THE TRIUMPH* – again, this is decision time and that means our emotional components come forward.

- **10% of the story:** *THE SAGE GUIDE* – we will spend just a little time reinforcing for them why we are the right ones to be their Sage Guide.

- **10% of the story:** *THE DISCOVERIES* – these get less emphasis because they were carefully contemplated in the prior stage.

- **10% of the story:** *THE VILLAIN* – when we get this far down in the journey, this component starts to take a back seat.

Review

When they get to Review, the question is, "Was this a good decision?" While how we are their *SAGE GUIDE* and *THE DISCOVERIES* are considered, this is less of a time for rational evaluation. *THE TRIUMPH* and *THE TRANSFORMATION* get the lion's share of the attention. Once again, *THE VILLAIN* gets less attention here as well.

Here is how much of this story we dedicate to each component:

- **40% of our story:** *THE TRANSFORMATION* –

this is an opportunity to remind our new customers that they are part of making a profound difference for those around them.

- **30% of the story:** *THE TRIUMPH* – this is the other emotional component that helps reinforce that our new customers made a good decision.

- **10% of the story:** *THE SAGE GUIDE* – we may want to remind our new customers of why they chose us, but it definitely takes a back seat to the emotional components.

- **10% of the story:** *THE DISCOVERIES* – again, we may want to briefly touch on everything that they have bought into.

- **10% of the story:** *THE VILLAIN* – we may want to remind them why this decision is relevant, but it definitely is not a priority.

Advocate

At the final stage, the question is, "Shouldn't others know about this?" This is that much coveted state where our customers become our advocates and evangelists. Here, we hope for them to spread our inspirational story. So, *THE TRANSFORMATION* receives much of the attention. It's not unusual that it would be supported by *THE TRIUMPH* as well. This is less of a time for the rational facts. This is a time for sharing something uplifting. For that reason, *THE SAGE GUIDE, THE DISCOVERIES* and *THE VILLAIN* play more of a support role.

Here is how much of this story we dedicate to each component:

- **50% of our story:** *THE TRANSFORMATION* – this is a call for our advocates to share this inspiring story with the world.

- **20% of the story:** *THE TRIUMPH* – this helps our advocates understand how to share the story in a way that is relevant as well as inspiring.

- **20% of the story:** *THE VILLAIN* – this helps our advocates illustrate the challenge that our solution so deftly addresses

- **5% of the story:** *THE SAGE GUIDE* – this is a support component at this stage.

- **5% of the story:** *THE DISCOVERIES* – this, too, is a support component at this stage

Note that our Big Audacious Meaning is present across all stages of the journey. Even at the stage where it has the least presence (Evaluation) it still has significant weight. We can't lose sight of its importance. It is what transforms lives. Transforms us. And transforms our stories.

There are a myriad of story possibilities – all driven by understanding the stages of our customers' journey and the importance of each of the story components at each of those stages. Be sure to check out the visual representation of the story framework at each stage of the journey in the Thrust Story Composition – available at dansalva.com/resources.

But make no mistake. This is not a formulaic process. With these story-building exercises, it can be too easy to believe that great stories are a matter of ordering the components correctly and making sure the ratio of words matches the formula for that stage. It doesn't work that way. Writing a compelling story is not formulaic. Writing a great story is an art. It is an emotional endeavor.

The rational structure I have laid out here has a role. It gives us clarity about what to write. It gives us guideposts to stay on the right path. That satisfies the rational part of our brain. Which may be the single most important role of this structure. Because once we satisfy the rational part of our brain, it clears the way for the emotional part of our brain to work its magic with our stories.

Key Takeaways

- There are 6 stages we all go through in our engagement with any organization: Define, Discover, Evaluate, Decide, Review, and Advocate. This is the customer journey.

- The story we tell is quite different at each of these stages. All the components are the same from story to story. It is how we order them and the time we spend on each that makes each story unique.

- Our Big Audacious Meaning is present across all stages of the journey. Even at the stage where it has the least presence (Evaluation) it still has significant weight. We can't lose sight of its importance.

- There are a myriad of story possibilities – all driven by understanding the stages of our customers' journey and the importance of each of the story components at each of those stages.

- This is not a formulaic process. The rational structure gives us clarity about what to write. It gives us guideposts to stay on the right path. And it clears the way for the emotional part of our brain to work its magic with our stories.

CHAPTER 16
Discovering the magic

Over the decades, I have worked on a broad range of clients and projects. Some more successful than others. I started to notice a pattern. There were certain clients and projects that were easier than others. These presented the best opportunities to do the most impactful work, and not surprisingly, ended up being the most successful efforts.

What set these special cases apart? These clients understood that they needed to do more than get someone to think about their offering. They understood that they needed people to feel something. To care.

Think about those companies that assail us with their features. Yes, I'm looking at you car manufacturers. Sport-tuned suspension. Navigation systems. Etc.

Don't get me wrong. There is a place for this. If you are in the market for a car, you may be comparing features. Especially if you're considering your choices. This is one of the stages of the customer journey.

The trouble is, the evaluation stage is just one of the 6 stages. Furthermore, it's the only part of the journey where the rational may take precedence over the emotional. It's not even the stage where the decision is made (the emotional takes over at this point).

So why invest millions in mass media to only appeal to one-sixth of the customer journey? Because listing the features feels logical. Rational. Safe. And it's easier to do research around the preference of features rather than the more nuanced subject of why prospects might care.

So we get assaulted with features. And find ourselves having a hard time finding a reason to care.

Sensational vs. substantial

About four years into my career, I had the chance to oversee the work on my state's lottery account. For a young guy working as a writer at an agency, this was exciting. The product was about fun and the thrill of maybe winning big. You could do some crazy stuff, as long as you could convince the client to buy it. As creatively freeing as that sounds, it bugged me.

Our teams would come up with ideas to promote the latest game. Sometimes the ideas were just off the wall. They didn't have anything to do with the game. They were just meant to get attention by being outrageous. I often found myself asking, "What does this mean?" After awhile, people on my team would tease me, knowing I was going to ask, "What does this mean?"

Crazy stunts. Wacky characters. That stuff can get you noticed. As a young guy in the business, I had doubts. Maybe I was overthinking this. Maybe it just needed to be crazy and cool.

The trouble is that it doesn't have staying power.

I had a team member who argued that our first job was to spark interest. I agree. But if there is no meaning behind it, there's no reason to care. And if we want them to make a buying decision (again and again), we have to give them a reason to care.

This doesn't mean that we abandon the crazy stuff. The unexpected. It just means that we have to have meaning with it as well. I won't kid you. That's difficult. It's easy to do something crazy for crazy's sake. But it takes talent to find the meaning and then find an unexpected way to bring it to life.

Looking back, I now know my instinct was right. There has to be more than just sensationalism.

Really great and captivating ideas are a rare commodity. There is a secret to increasing the potential for creating these kind of impactful ideas. It's a Big Audacious Meaning. It creates fertile ground for cultivating endless compelling ways to connect with our prospects and customers. Because a Big Audacious Meaning is bold, emotional, and irresistible. That is the ideal place to start if we're looking to create ideas that move people.

But we need to consider something else as well. It's not just the story we tell, but the way we tell it. It can make a difference in how quickly our Big Audacious Meaning spreads.

To truly unleash that game-changing purpose-driven story, we need to understand those things that will amplify how we tell that story.

Unleashing our purpose-driven story: start with humility

Humility gives us the ability to put our needs aside and serve those of our fellow human beings. This becomes essential as we create our stories.

Developing genuine humility causes another pretty wonderful thing to happen. It can bring down the natural defenses of others.

There is a apprehension we all have about being judged. When one of us demonstrates genuine humility, it helps everyone let go of that fear. Usually it is with loved ones that we feel this comfortable. We feel like we can be ourselves – warts and all. Now imagine fostering that feeling for everyone we engage. Think about what that could do. Imagine a group of people feeling that comfortable around us.

If we want to bring people together and make them feel confident and optimistic, humility is our ticket to getting there.

Of course, humility can get interpreted as weakness. It can be misconstrued as meekness or a lack of confidence. But truly great leaders show humility. Unfortunately, humility doesn't get much attention in today's world. Rather it's the self-promoting, blustering personalities that grab headlines.

A great way of understanding the power of humility is to look at what happens in its absence.

Often what we consider strong leadership is nothing more than hubris. Hubris is a showing of excessive pride or self-confidence. It's easy to be fooled by leaders who seem so sure of their view of the world and their decisions. Their excessive confidence causes people to be convinced of their ability.

Take Enron for example – one of the most insidious corporate debacles in recent history. It led to the largest bankruptcy reorganization of its time. The incredible arrogance of the leadership resulted in scores of people not only losing their jobs, but also losing their retirement savings. Maybe the only sense of justice in all this is that those leaders ended up going to jail. It is a cautionary tale about danger of hubris.

Humility inoculates us against this hubris. But perhaps the most desirable thing about humility is its ability to help us become the best version of ourselves. It's interesting that the way to do this very personal thing is to do something that feels almost contrary. To not focus on ourselves, but to focus on others. As C.S. Lewis once said, "True humility is not thinking less of yourself; it is thinking of yourself less."

After all, when we're thinking about others we don't have the capacity to be obsessing over our needs. Scheming about how we will get others to do what we want.

In short, humility brings out the best in us. And that creates fertile ground for our stories to flourish.

Unleashing our purpose-driven story: adding in empathy

While humility guides how we act, it could be argued that empathy defines how we interact. With empathy, we hope to understand others and feel what they feel. Then we use that newfound insight to guide how we interact with others. That interaction can be everything from a one-to-one relationship to a product we develop.

As my kids were growing up, it was important to my wife and me that they understand and develop a sense of empathy for those around them. It was our belief that empathy would help them not only be good human beings, but also help them become intuitive problem solvers.

For me, empathy was the most important skill I hoped that they would learn (not that we didn't have many a stern conversation concerning math, English, etc.) I use the word 'skill' intentionally here. I believe that while we're all endowed with the ability to empathize (unless, of course, you're a sociopath), ultimately empathy must be practiced and honed.

It's easy to believe we are practicing empathy when really, it's just sympathy we're expressing. Sympathy is us feeling sorry for someone. It can be conveyed in a greeting card with a sentiment like, "I'm sorry for your loss." But empathy is too nuanced to be captured with a one-liner. Empathy requires more of us. Because having true empathy means attempting to understand how a fellow human being feels. That means stepping into her shoes and walking a mile or two.

Empathy is about respect. A respect that allows us to subordinate our own agenda, and focus on the needs of others. It requires a dedication to our fellow man (or woman). We have to listen and learn. We have to suspend our own agenda. We have to dedicate ourselves to helping them discover how to accomplish their goals.

That takes a servant's heart. If we're interrupting people to tell them how to solve their problem, it's a good bet that we need to work on our empathy.

Mastering empathy is quickly becoming a lost ability. Today's hectic pace makes it challenging to take time to really understand someone and develop genuine empathy. Which may explain why it seems to be in short supply.

But empathy can help us do some pretty great things. For starters, it helps us to connect with others because it telegraphs that we are honestly attempting to relate to them. More impressively, it can help us develop groundbreaking stories. When we truly understand those we're serving, we can create things that really get to the heart of their need. More than that, it allows us to do it in a way that respects and preserves the dignity of those we are serving.

Have you ever had that feeling that a product, service, or experience was designed specifically for you? It's like someone climbed inside your head, figured out what was important, and then created something that felt incredibly relevant and personal. You can bet that when this product/experience/story was developed, it was done with great empathy.

These are the kind of stories that win hearts as well as minds. They are the things that get talked about, and recommended. In fact, when stories create advocates or even evangelists, it's safe to assume there is a great sense of empathy at the core.

If we really want to make a difference, we must have a genuine understanding of what those we hope to serve face and how they feel. That's no easy task. But that is what makes it so worthwhile. There is no greater feeling than to know that we have made a significant difference for another.

Our Big Audacious Meaning is founded in the difference we will make for others. Empathy was a key part of its creation. By developing this deep empathy for all those we hope to serve, we can increase our ability to successfully introduce the story of our Big Audacious Meaning and speed the adoption.

Unleashing our purpose-driven story: embracing wonder

Cynicism can be useful. It can help us do a reality check when it seems that everyone is drinking the Kool-Aid. But it can also be a dangerous crutch. It's easy to be cynical. It doesn't take any emotional investment. It doesn't require that we put ourselves out there, vulnerable to criticism. As such, it can be an innovation killer.

When we're preparing to create our stories, cynicism can be the anchor that drags along the bottom, slowing us to a snail's pace (okay, a sea snail – just to stay with the nautical theme.)

This is why a sense of wonder is crucial.

Wonder is the ability to look at the world through childlike eyes. It's the ability to find amazement in what others may see as mundane things. It's an incredible innocence that opens us up to the world.

When we were kids, we were full of the stuff. Life then was filled with discovery. Backyard expeditions. Amazing things just around the corner. Life was wonder-full.

Somewhere along the way, we got in a big hurry to grow up. Christopher Robin leaves the hundred acre woods. Peter Pan trades in his sword for a briefcase and career ambition.

And we were willing to let the wonder go in what seemed like a fair trade to pursue this new adventure. 'Adulting' as my twentysomething kids would say.

But it wasn't a fair trade. The price was too much to ask. We too quickly left behind something that was more valuable than we could ever realize.

We live in a data-driven frenzy. We can parse and measure our actions with unprecedented speed and accuracy. We quantify our every move. And use it to define the world we now inhabit.

This isn't to say that all this hasn't had great benefit. It has. That's not the point. It's not a judgment of what we have gained in our advancement. Rather, it is question of what may be overshadowed by the technological strides that we continue to take at an accelerating pace. It is a question of what we may be pushing aside.

In the mad rush to quantify our every move, we may be giving up a little too much of our humanity. We may be leaving wonder behind.

We don't often think about the value of wonder. There is

no metric to evaluate its contribution. So grizzled leadership teams dismiss it as a baseless factor. It becomes some messy and emotional unknown that makes everyone a little uncomfortable because we can't put it on a spreadsheet.

Yet, think about those moments when a business - a cold and unemotional entity - has brought us to the brink of tears. Or shared a thought that has made our hearts skip a beat. Taken our breath away. Or, given us goose bumps. At the core of those experiences is wonder.

It could be a something that shakes us out of our malaise and reintroduces us to a little bit of the magic in the world around us. It could be a thought that helps us rediscover something revelatory about the relationships we share. Whatever it is, it opens our eyes and helps us return to that state of wonder that we lost, yet we are so desperately drawn to.

These are the moments that organizations desire. They want us to have a visceral reaction at the very mention of their names. They want us to become fans, advocates, and even evangelists for them.

That kind of feeling doesn't emerge from a spreadsheet. It doesn't magically appear when we recite our litany of features. It arises when we reconnect humans with that thing that we are all longing for. A sense of wonder.

Wonder helps spark two pretty awesome things. Inspiration and optimism.

Without wonder, it's impossible to open ourselves up to the really inspiring possibilities that we could embrace. Wonder helps us see the world without the restraints of cynicism. It frees us to explore areas we may have fenced off or discover things we may have overlooked. Imagine a brand aligning itself with the good things to come or reconnecting us with those forgotten things that bring us real joy. If we desire game changing ideas, then we must find the courage to allow ourselves to embrace a sense of wonder.

Then there is optimism. Wonder engenders an incredible positivity. Just spend some time with any 6 year old. Kids have an amazing positivity about them. It's no coincidence that they also have an incredible sense of wonder. They go hand in hand.

Optimism is a powerful force. It can help us envision greater things. It can strengthen resolve. Most of all, it can unleash enthusiasm and energy. That's the kind of thing that can transform prospects into evangelists. And help an entire organization do some pretty amazing things.

Returning to a state of wonder is no easy chore. The idea of it may run counter to the way we have lived our business lives over the years or even decades. But there are a myriad of ways for an organization to foster it. Exploring mindfulness has become a trending method.[51]

Practicing gratitude is also a way to ground ourselves and open the door to wonder. There are plenty of other approaches as well.[52]

It doesn't take too much searching to uncover all kinds of ideas you can put to use.

But, recognize this. Wonder is fragile. If an organization is going to harness its power, it has to believe in it. It has to nurture it. Cynicism can crush it. Indifference is just as dangerous (leaders who don't buy in can kill it by just going through the motions.) It takes strong leaders to help everyone believe that their sense of wonder is valuable. And powerful.

Help everyone believe that and you'll find yourself in awe of what you have created.

Igniting humility, empathy, and wonder

When I was kid, we would invariably get that one assignment. I remember Sister Ruth standing in front of a room full of us fifth graders. All 5' 1" of her dressed in her blue nun's habit. She would say, "Tell me what you're thankful for."

I would fill the page with things like, "I'm thankful for mom, and dad, and grandma and grandpa. I'm thankful for my house. And snow days. And Pepper (the wonder schnauzer)."

It seemed effortless to reel off a litany of blessings.

The years rolled by. Sister Ruth was no longer around requiring me to enumerate my gratitude. The litany faded.

It seems obvious. Of course we should appreciate the world around us, including all those that inhabit it. That's just part of being a good human. It may be one of those things that's so obvious that we overlook the importance of actually putting it into practice. And putting it into practice is important. Because, beyond being a good human, gratitude does some pretty wonderful stuff for us.

Humility goes hand-in-hand with thankfulness. In order to be sincerely thankful, we have to be humble. It's hard to be self-aggrandizing when we're recognizing that there's some higher power involved in our success. The very nature of feeling thankful for all that we have helps us adopt a sense of humility.

Thankfulness also encourages empathy. It helps us be more considerate toward others. Expressing gratitude makes us more cognizant of how others may feel and what they may be going through in their lives. It makes us consider our interconnectedness.

It helps shift our thinking, making it less about 'me' and more about 'we'.

Amplifying our sense of wonder may be one of the most magical things about thankfulness. Thankfulness helps us stop and really take a look around. Being grateful puts us in a state that allows us to really see those amazing things that surround us. They are usually simple, unassuming things that don't scream for attention. But as we take the time to notice, we find ourselves awed by the beauty. Awed by the complexity that makes it all possible. It's seeing the extraordinary in the ordinary. It's an incredible feeling to be overcome by that kind of wonder.

There is no one way that thankfulness absolutely must be practiced. It could be everything from recounting our blessings at the end of the day to incorporating it into daily meditation.

For me, it starts with my morning drive to work. I have made it a habit to say out loud, "Thank you for this beautiful day." Is that a bit over the top? Maybe for some. What I've found is that it's not just about saying those 6 words. It's what happens afterward. Those words reorient my line of thought. It sends me down a path and I find myself thinking more deeply about being thankful. It's irresistible. Because with those thoughts of gratitude come a genuine feeling of happiness.

Most remarkably, those feelings sustain and I find myself thinking about thankfulness more often. A post on Inc. pointed to a recent study that confirms this phenomenon.[53]

I'm still a little surprised at myself as I say my 6 words each day. I find it irresistible to surrender myself to the feeling of thankfulness. Is it brain chemistry? Or something more spiritual (maybe it's the ghost of Sister Ruth?) I'm not really sure. I do know this: when I'm thinking about gratitude, I find myself feeling full of hope. There is very little room in my thoughts for cynicism. Very little room for worry. That's a pretty remarkable feeling. To be thankful.

A thankfulness epidemic?

I was working with one organization that would start every meeting with a prayer. The prayer would thank God for everything good the organization had and ask for a productive meeting.

Everybody approaches their beliefs differently. I tend to be more private with mine. So this pre-meeting ritual was a little bit uncomfortable for me at first. But after a while, I began to look forward to the prayer. It made me stop thinking about all my worries and focus on how I could become a better contributor to those around me. It made me take stock of the progress that had been made (something I too often forget to reflect on). That changed things for me. It also changed the tone of whatever meeting I was in. It shifted from a meeting to fix problems to one where we were exploring ways to build on successes. Which type of meeting would you rather be part of? Yeah, me too.

There was also this other benefit that came out of that pre-meeting thanks giving. You see, it's hard to be a bully or a jerk in a meeting after praying together with your fellow attendees. No, really. Give it a try. If you don't curb your self-focused, aggressive behavior, there will be a higher likelihood that the group will do it for you. I saw it happen. It's a pretty wonderful thing.

I don't think you have to ask everyone to pray to introduce thankfulness. It could be some simple mindfulness practices. Like asking everyone to be in the moment (no checking your phone or laptop) and then taking one minute for everyone to silently meditate on what they are thankful for before diving into the agenda.

If that's too touchy-feely, simply start by reviewing all the progress made to date and recognizing everyone for their contributions toward making it happen. Even this little bit of thankfulness will make a difference.

Here is the really irresistible thing. Any little bit of thankfulness is likely to spread. After all, it's contagious. Thanking one person makes it more likely that they will thank another in turn. Heck, if we do it enough, it could cause a whole thankfulness epidemic. Imagine that spreading through the organization. Through the population.

At the very least, it would cause us to dread some of our meetings a little less. And at the very most, well, who knows? We may find ourselves helping to spread something that makes a real difference in our world. Just by being thankful. It's infectious just to think about.

If we allow gratitude to ignite our humility, empathy, and wonder, we become better. Better able to clarify our Big Audacious Meaning. And better able to discover the power to unleash our purpose-driven story.

A story with Big Audacious Meaning

Great stories are full of magic and wonder. I'm not talking about the Harry Potter-esque treatment. I'm talking about the kind of awe that we feel when we hear a story that helps us feel like we can be part of something larger than ourselves. Something that can make a difference for another person. Or something that can make the world around us a little bit better place. Those are the stories every brand should aspire to tell.

That's not the exclusive territory of darling brands. We all have the ability to embrace that transformative ideal – that purpose that will form the core of our story, turning what was previously serviceable into something that has the potential to inspire everyone we hope to serve.

Hopefully, this book has helped demonstrate how we all have this ability. We can clarify a Big Audacious Meaning no matter what type of organization we work with. Then we can take that Big Audacious Meaning and bring it into our story through the Thrust Story Framework.

That can do something pretty extraordinary.

It can help us discover that, what we do everyday, can make a difference in a life. A community. Or even the world.

It can transform our organization. It can transform us.

The story of our Big Audacious Meaning is waiting to be told.

Key Takeaways

- Humility gives us the ability to put our needs aside and serve those of our fellow human beings. It brings out the best in us. And that creates fertile ground for our stories to flourish.

- Empathy is about subordinating our own agenda, and focusing on the needs of others. By developing this deep empathy, we can increase our ability to successfully introduce the story of our Big Audacious Meaning and speed the adoption.

- Wonder helps us see the world without the restraints of cynicism. It frees us to explore areas we may have fenced off or discover things we may have overlooked.

- If we allow gratitude to ignite our humility, empathy, and wonder, we become better able to clarify our Big Audacious Meaning. And better able to discover the power to unleash our purpose-driven story.

- Great stories are full of magic and wonder. They help us feel like we can be part of something that can make the world around us a little bit better place. Those are the stories every brand should aspire to tell.

EPILOGUE

When I was a kid, a job was a job. And getting one wasn't anything more than a way to make a few bucks. A source of capital, if you will, to help fund my efforts during non-work hours to see just what kind of shenanigans I could get into.

That was satisfying for a while. But eventually, the shenanigans got old. I felt the need to find something more compelling. So I headed off to college to discover what I was called to do. And lo and behold, I came out on the other side of those years with a pretty solid idea of the career I wanted to pursue. It was in the marketing and advertising field.

Now I know that working in advertising doesn't sound like an incredibly noble pursuit. But there was something that drew me to it. I didn't actually study advertising in college. I was a journalism major (broadcast news). So much of the way I approached my work was influenced by that. I wanted to find that thing that needed to be told. That thing that would be valuable to those who I hoped to serve.

When I started working in the advertising field, I quickly decided I didn't like the reputation my industry had. Not that it wasn't deserved. There were (and still are) a lot of cheesy, gimmick-driven practitioners out there that call themselves advertising professionals. They are just a shade shy of snake oil salesmen. And by a "shade shy", I mean they aren't even that ethical. But I digress.

The thing is, I didn't feel like some huckster. I believed that I could make a difference for somebody. For me, it wasn't about doing anything at all costs to get a prospect's attention. It was more about providing something of value. Something that would help somebody make a decision. Maybe make something a little clearer. Or, help them discover something helpful that they didn't know existed.

Was that naive? Maybe so. But it is what I believed. And it showed up in my work.

I was always looking to create something that would help. Something that would inspire. Oh, I didn't always get stellar results. But the vast majority of efforts were successful. And they lined up with a belief that helping is the most powerful form of promotion there is. Because it doesn't just grab attention - it creates believers.

This didn't happen overnight. Like most worthwhile efforts, it involved a journey.

It evolved out of a love for great branding. The kind of branding that connects on an emotional level. You've experienced it. It's the kind of stuff that causes people to willing wear a company's logo on their shirt (and I'm not just talking about the logos of sportswear companies.) It emerges in a story that gives you goose bumps as you watch or read it.

Naturally, I loved great storytelling. Especially when the authors gave us a way to think about something in a way that we had not imagined. But I also learned throughout my career that just having a talented storyteller was not enough. Early on, I thought I could get by with just great storytelling. I would be handed an assignment where nothing special had been identified about the brand. I thought I could still make it work by inventing an interesting story.

And that's what I delivered. An interesting premise that would capture attention. But every time, these stories just wouldn't stick with people. They dissolved away. Like cotton candy. Because there was nothing beyond the clever story. There was no depth.

My solution was to dive into strategy. I figured that if a storyteller could become really good at strategy, he could unlock the secret to those great stories. I pushed myself to become that person who could lay out a differentiating strategic framework and then apply my storytelling skills to bring that strategy to life in an unexpected and compelling way.

The stories got better. But they still were not consistently the goose bumps-inducing gems that made me want to get into this business in the first place.

Something was still missing.

As I looked back over my career, I wanted to believe there was some overlooked clue to what made great brand stories great. I separated out those stories that reached that rarified level. Goose bumps status. What made those efforts so successful? Was it just random good fortune? There were lots of differences between the projects. But they didn't seem to have any secret ingredient that united all of them.

This was frustrating. I didn't want to admit that sometimes things just work out. That telling great stories was determined by the whims of fate. I had to be missing something.

My problem was that I was looking in the wrong place. I was examining the way that features were combined. Studying how benefits were built. These were important things to understand. But they were also keeping me from really understanding what made for great stories.

Maybe it was because I was getting older. Maybe it was because I had spent a lot of years in this business – and I was becoming jaded. Whatever the reason, I really started thinking about what I was doing.

I thought, "Is this how I wanted to spend my time?" Because time becomes more precious as you get older. Something started to occur to me. It wasn't just about telling great stories. It was about telling stories that could make a profound difference for someone. Stories that brashly believed that they could help an individual. Or a community. Or even the world.

I got really excited about that idea. And then immediately thought it was all just too presumptuous. I worried that people would laugh me out of the room if I said I wanted to tell stories that helped change lives. I put it aside.

But it would not stay there.

I started thinking a lot about us as humans and how important stories are to everything from preserving history to teaching morals to inspiring change. That last one tugged at me. Change starts as a story.

This is when I started to understand what made great stories great. It was purpose.

When a brand or an organization embraced a Big Audacious Meaning, magical things happened. I went back to that collection of stories that I had compiled. And sure enough, it became evident. The common denominator was purpose.

I still live for telling great stories. But now I know that the story alone is not enough.

I know there is something that we must clarify first. We must uncover, unlock, and unleash that thing that ignites passions. That thing that brings the goose bumps.

Probably the most interesting outcome of all this is that it changed work for me. Just believing I could make a difference got me excited about what I was doing. I felt like I was contributing. I found a real passion. Because I felt like I had a purpose. Although, at the time, I didn't call it that.

Today, it's much clearer to me. I find myself talking to organizations about a Big Audacious Meaning - the profound difference we can make in a life, a community, or even the world. It's incredibly rewarding to see those organizations embrace a purpose. And then to see what it can mean for team members, for customers, for prospects and more. It is an incredible feeling to be part of that journey. Looking back to when I was a kid and getting my first job, I never imagined that work could feel that way. That it could feel like more than a way to just make a few bucks. That it could feel like a pursuit. Like a pretty worthwhile way to spend the days. That it could feel purposeful.

For more about Big Audacious Meaning, visit: dansalva.com.

To inquire about speaking engagements, workshops, and consulting, email dsalva@dansalva.com

THANKS

First and foremost, thank you to my Mom and Dad. Their love and support continues to be fundamental to who I am.

Thank you to everyone who offered to read the book in its raw form. The effort and comments were much appreciated. A special thank you to Kim Sharan and Mark Rieger for their insights. They helped me make this a better book.

Most of all, thank you to my wife, Amy. Her patience with me is inexplicable. And her encouragement helped me more than she will ever know. When it all felt like a fool's errand, it was her kind words that kept me going.

And lastly, thank you for reading this far. We can spread a little more goodness in our world. Together, we can set off a chain reaction of organizations and individuals making a difference for the people around them. It all starts with a Big Audacious Meaning.

ABOUT THE AUTHOR

Dan Salva is an author and builder of brands with experience that stretches over three decades and covers architecting and executing purpose-driven brand experiences for regional, national, and international organizations.

He shares what he's learned over time to help organizations revolutionize their success by embracing one of today's most exciting strategic opportunities – unleashing a purpose-driven brand story to amplify the impact they can have on lives, communities, and even the world.

Dan received dual degrees from the University of Missouri-Columbia. And, over the years, co-founded three companies, including Will & Grail – a brand innovation firm. Today he helps organizations clarify their Big Audacious Meaning and then bring it into their story to transform their success.

Dan lives just outside of Kansas City in the burgeoning epicenter of purpose-driven brand thinking – Sugar Creek, Missouri. He has been married to his wife Amy longer than he would have guessed she would have stuck around. They have three sons – Mitch, Jack, and Andy - who promise not to make fun of their dear old dad but, evidently, are pretty lousy at keeping promises. Other than that, they are generally regarded as being awesome.

ENDNOTES

1   Percy, Ian. The Profitable Power of Purpose. Scottsdale, Arizona: Inspired Productions Press, LLC, 2004.

2   Collins, Jim, and Jerry I. Porras. Built to Last: Successful Habits of Visionary Companies . New York, New York: Harper Business, 1994.

3   "Definition of Purpose." Purpose | Definition of Purpose. Accessed February 26, 2018. https://www.merriam-webster.com/dictionary/purpose.

4   Spary, Sara. "Unilever says 'brands with purpose' are growing at twice the speed of others in portfolio." May 5, 2015. Accessed February 26, 2018. http://www.marketingmagazine.co.uk/article/1345772/unilever-says-brands-purpose-growing-twice-speed-others-portfolio.

5   Adams, James Truslow. The Epic of America. Boston, Massachusetts: Little Brown & Company, 1931.

6   Adkins, Amy. "Millennials: The Job-Hopping Generation." Gallup.com. May 12, 2016. Accessed February 26, 2018. http://news.gallup.com/businessjournal/191459/millennials-job-hopping-generation.aspx.

7   Fottrell, Quentin. "American workers are burned
     out and overworked." MarketWatch. June 30, 2015.
     Accessed March 03, 2018. http://www.marketwatch.
     com/story/american-workers-are-burned-out-and-
     overworked-2015-06-30.

8   "USC CTM Releases Report on Americans' Media
     Consumption." USC Marshall. October 28, 2013. Accessed
     March 03, 2018. https://www.marshall.usc.edu/news/
     usc-ctm-releases-report-americans-media-consumption.

9   Karlin, Susan. "Earth's Nervous System: Looking At
     Humanity Through Big Data." Fast Company. November
     28, 2012. Accessed March 03, 2018. https://www.
     fastcompany.com/1681986/earth-s-nervous-system-
     looking-at-humanity-through-big-data.

10   Levitin, Daniel J. The organized mind: thinking straight in
     the age of information overload. New York: Dutton, 2016.

11   Hemp, Paul. "Death by Information Overload." Harvard
     Business Review. July 31, 2014. Accessed February 26,
     2018. https://hbr.org/2009/09/death-by-information-
     overload.

12   Kahneman, Daniel. Thinking, fast and slow. New York:
     Farrar, Straus and Giroux, 2015.

13   "Attention Span Statistics." Attention Span Statistics - Statistic Brain. July 2, 2016. Accessed February 26, 2018. https://www.statisticbrain.com/attention-span-statistics/.

14   Percy, Ian. The Profitable Power of Purpose. Scottsdale, Arizona: Inspired Productions Press, LLC, 2004.

15   Schiller, Ben. "Understanding The Purpose-Driven Worker (And Why It's Okay If You're Not One)." Fast Company. August 23, 2016. Accessed March 03, 2018. https://www.fastcoexist.com/3063039/understanding-the-purpose-driven-worker-and-why-its-ok-if-youre-not-one.

16   Terkle, Studs. Working: People Talk About What They Do All Day and How They Feel About What They Do. New York, New York: The New Press, 1997.

17   Collins, Jim, and Jerry I. Porras. Built to Last: Successful Habits of Visionary Companies . New York, New York: Harper Business, 1994.

18   Kahneman, Daniel. Thinking, fast and slow. New York: Farrar, Straus and Giroux, 2015.

19   Ariely, Dan. "The Miata scenario, or justifying what we desire." PBS. June 28, 2011. Accessed March 03, 2018. http://www.pbs.org/wnet/need-to-know/opinion/the-miata-scenario-or-justifying-what-we-desire/10134/.

20   Graves, Christopher. "Part One: "We Are Not Thinking Machines. We Are Feeling Machines That Think."." Institute for Public Relations. March 17, 2015. Accessed March 03, 2018. https://instituteforpr.org/part-one-not-thinking-machines-feeling-machines-think/.

21   The Sustainability Imperative - New insights on consumer expectations. The Nielsen Company. October 2015. Accessed February 26, 2018. https://www.nielsen.com/content/dam/nielsenglobal/dk/docs/global-sustainability-report-oct-2015.pdf.

22   "Culture of purpose | Deloitte US | Building business confidence." Deloitte United States. May 22, 2017. Accessed March 03, 2018. https://www2.deloitte.com/us/en/pages/about-deloitte/articles/culture-of-purpose.html.

23   Spence, Roy M., Jr. It's Not What You Sell, It's What You Stand For: Why Every Extraordinary Business Is Driven by Purpose. New York, New York: Penguin Random House, 2011.

24 Kotter, John P. Corporate culture and performance. New York, New York: SIMON AND SCHUSTER, 2011.

25 Sisodia, Rajendra, David B. Wolfe, and Jagdish N. Sheth. Firms of endearment: the pursuit of purpose and profit. Upper Saddle River, NJ, New Jersey: Pearson Education, 2007.

26 Rosenberg, Yuval. "Measured Progress." Measured Progress. April 01, 2007. Accessed February 26, 2018. https://www.fastcompany.com/59230/measured-progress.

27 Mainwaring, Simon. "Marketing 3.0 Will Be Won By Purpose-Driven, Social Brands [Infographic]." Forbes. July 16, 2013. Accessed March 03, 2018. https://www.forbes.com/sites/simonmainwaring/2013/07/16/marketing-3-0-will-be-won-by-purpose-driven-social-brands-infographic/#5478bd4d1886.

28 Jones, Bruce. "Talking Point: The Disney Institute Blog." Why Organizations Must Create Emotional Service Experiences | Talking Point | The Disney Institute Blog. July 25, 2013. Accessed March 03, 2018. https://disneyinstitute.com/blog/2013/07/why-organizations-must-create-emotional-service-experiences.

29   Heath, Chip, and Dan Heath. Made to Stick: Why Some
      Ideas Survive and Others Die. New York, New York:
      Random House Books, 2007.

30   Lazonick, William, Gautam Mukunda, and Dominic
      Barton. "Profits Without Prosperity." Harvard Business
      Review. September 2014. Accessed March 03, 2018.
      https://hbr.org/2014/09/profits-without-prosperity.

31   Reiman, Joey. The story of purpose: the path to creating
      a brighter brand, a greater company, and a lasting legacy.
      Hoboken, NJ: Wiley, 2013.

32   Pink, Daniel H. Drive: the surprising truth about what
      motivates us. New York, NY: Riverhead Books, 2012.

33   "Dove." Dove | Brand | Unilever Global Company Website.
      Accessed February 28, 2018. https://www.unilever.com/
      brands/our-brands/dove.html.

34   "About Dove." Dove | About Dove. Accessed February 28,
      2018. https://www.dove.com/us/en/stories/about-dove.html.

35   "Our research." Our Research | Dove. Accessed February
      28, 2018. https://www.dove.com/us/en/stories/about-dove/
      our-research.html.

36   Hurst, Aaron. The purpose economy: how your desire for impact, personal growth and community is changing the world. Boise, ID: Elevate, USA, 2016.

37   "The Business Case For Purpose." The business case for purpose. http://www.ey.com/Publication/vwLUAssets/ ey-the-business-case-for-purpose/$FILE/ey-the-business-case-for-purpose.pdf.

38   EY. Transformation Trends. Accessed February 28, 2018. http://www.ey.com/Publication/vwLUAssets/EY-about-purpose-and-business/$FILE/EY-about-purpose-and-business.pdf.

39   Collins, Jim, and Jerry I. Porras. Built to Last: Successful Habits of Visionary Companies . New York, New York: Harper Business, 1994.

40   Mackey, John, and Rajendra Sisodia. Conscious capitalism: liberating the heroic spirit of business. Boston, MA: Harvard Business Review Press, 2014.

41   Heath, Chip, and Dan Heath. Made to Stick: Why Some Ideas Survive and Others Die. New York, New York: Random House Books, 2007.

42   "Our mission." Mission Statement | Starbucks Coffee Company. Accessed February 28, 2018. https://www. starbucks.com/about-us/company-information/mission-statement.

43   Cooper, Belle Beth. "Why People Don't Buy Products– They Buy Better Versions Of Themselves." Fast Company. January 28, 2014. Accessed March 03, 2018. https://www. fastcompany.com/3025484/why-people-dont-buy-products-they-buy-better-versions-of-themselves.

44   Reiman, Joey. The story of purpose: the path to creating a brighter brand, a greater company, and a lasting legacy. Hoboken, NJ: Wiley, 2013.

45   Mackey, John, and Rajendra Sisodia. Conscious capitalism: liberating the heroic spirit of business. Boston, MA: Harvard Business Review Press, 2014.

46   McLeod, Lisa Earle. Leading with Noble Purpose: How to Create a Tribe of True Believers. Hoboken, New Jersey: John Wiley & Sons, 2016.

47   Zak, Paul J. "Why Your Brain Loves Good Storytelling." Harvard Business Review. October 28, 2014. Accessed March 03, 2018. https://hbr.org/2014/10/why-your-brain-loves-good-storytelling.

48   Sinek, Simon. Start with why: how great leaders inspire
       everyone to take action. London: Portfolio/Penguin, 2009.

49   Sinek, Simon. Start with why: how great leaders inspire
       everyone to take action. London: Portfolio/Penguin, 2009.

50   Campbell, Joseph. The hero with a thousand faces. 21st ed.
       Princeton, New Jersey: Princeton University Press, 1973.

51   Mayo Clinic Staff. "How to practice mindfulness." Mayo
       Clinic. November 10, 2015. Accessed March 03, 2018.
       http://www.mayoclinic.org/healthy-lifestyle/consumer-
       health/in-depth/mindfulness-exercises/art-20046356?pg=1.

52   Girard, Lisa. "How to Find Your Passion in 5 Creativity
       Exercises." Entrepreneur. June 02, 2011. Accessed March
       03, 2018. https://www.entrepreneur.com/article/219709.

53   Stillman, Jessica. "Gratitude Physically Changes Your
       Brain, New Study Says." Inc.com. Accessed March 03,
       2018. http://www.inc.com/jessica-stillman/the-amazing-
       way-gratitude-rewires-your-brain-for-happiness.html.